The Digital Pandemic

The Digital Pandemic
Imagination in Times of Isolation

JOÃO PEDRO CACHOPO

Translated by Rachael McGill

BLOOMSBURY ACADEMIC
LONDON · NEW YORK · OXFORD · NEW DELHI · SYDNEY

BLOOMSBURY ACADEMIC
Bloomsbury Publishing Plc
50 Bedford Square, London, WC1B 3DP, UK
1385 Broadway, New York, NY 10018, USA
29 Earlsfort Terrace, Dublin 2, Ireland

BLOOMSBURY, BLOOMSBURY ACADEMIC and the Diana logo
are trademarks of Bloomsbury Publishing Plc

First published in Great Britain 2022

This work is funded by national funds through the FCT – Fundação
para a Ciência e a Tecnologia, I.P., under the Norma
Transitória – DL 57/2016/CP1453/CT0059.

Cover design by Ben Anslow
Cover image: Top view of people walking in different directions of pattern,
painted on asphalt (© Klaus Vedfelt / Getty Images)

A catalogue record for this book is available from the British Library.

A catalog record for this book is available from the Library of Congress.

ISBN: HB: 978-1-3502-8428-9
         PB: 978-1-3502-8429-6
       ePDF: 978-1-3502-8432-6
      eBook: 978-1-3502-8430-2

Typeset by Integra Software Services Pvt. Ltd.
Printed and bound in Great Britain

To find out more about our authors and books visit www.bloomsbury.com
and sign up for our newsletters.

CONTENTS

ACKNOWLEDGEMENTS

A study of this sort, developed under these circumstances, could not be undertaken alone. I am grateful to everyone, near and far, with whom I shared and discussed, briefly or at length, the ideas explored in this book: Ana Ilievska, Dominique Mortiaux, Filipe Pinto, Gonçalo Marcelo, Jessica Di Chiara, João Oliveira Duarte, Kateryna Maksymova, Kelly Hecklinger, Luís Ferro, Maria Filomena Molder, Mariana Castro, Mariana Pinto dos Santos, Nuno Fonseca, Pedro Duarte, Sílvio Santana and Virginia de Araújo Figueiredo.

PROLOGUE

The pandemic is not the event

The title of this prologue defies common sense. Instead of pointing directly and unequivocally to the purpose of the book, it winks at it with a negative, provocatively elusive assertion: 'The pandemic is not the event'. In its irony, the title could be seen as misleading, but is it really so? Might the discomfort it elicits in the reader not be productive – generating a furtive and jumpy restlessness unbound from certainty? This same discomfort has troubled me since the first months of the pandemic: the sensation that what is happening is eluding us, the suspicion that the event preceded and will continue after the shock, that it is taking place on another plane and that, distracted by the clamour of the madness and wisdom of the times, we have not yet fully weighed the scale of the event or the extent of its consequences.

Too many questions remain. What type of event is the Covid-19 pandemic? How did we react to its outbreak at the beginning of 2020? What does this reaction reveal about the world in which we live? How is the pandemic transforming our lives? How can and should we position ourselves ethically, politically and artistically in the face of these changes? What is the relationship between the unfolding of the pandemic and the deepening of the climate crisis? What will become of us afterwards? This book's attempt to answer these questions rests on the hypothesis that the pandemic is not *in itself* the event. The event, precipitated by the conjunction of social distancing and the intensified use of digital technologies, is a disruption of the senses: a radical shift in how we imagine ourselves as close to or distant from all that surrounds us.

*

In early 2020 we were abruptly obligated to go into isolation, a consequence of the lockdown and social-distancing measures taken to contain the Covid-19 pandemic. The isolation was not absolute, and its imposition, sometimes stricter, sometimes more flexible, has varied greatly worldwide, according to personal, social and economic circumstances. The restrictions of a 'global quarantine' and the 'new normality' have led to the recurrent and prolonged use of digital technologies: devices, platforms and applications with the most diverse functionalities, but with the common purpose of remedying distance. None of these technologies was new, but their use has imposed itself on our lives with an unprecedented intensity. In more than one sense, digital remediation has proved to be a condition of possibility of experience, reconfiguring the topology of our lives. Confined to our homes, we imagined ourselves more distant to what was close and, at the same time, closer to what was distant.

The concept of 'remediation' will play a crucial role throughout this book. I want to clarify the reasons for privileging it over so many other concepts that would permit discussion of digital technologies and their intensified use during the pandemic. The first concerns the very definition of the term, introduced by Jay David Bolter and Richard Grusin in *Remediation: Understanding New Media* in 1999, as 'the representation of one medium in another'.[1] Although remediation has a complex genealogy, harking back to medieval illuminated manuscripts, the relevance of the concept in the contemporary world relates to the fact that it conveys what digital technology alone has made possible, due to the universality of its binary code: the systematic confluence of different media – sound, image and text – in a single medium. In this sense, remediation epitomizes the way in which digital media work, and it is in this sense that the concept is most often used in this book.

The second reason concerns the word's semantic ambivalence. In evoking the notions of remedy, relief and restoration, remediation suggests a reparative substitution. For all of its simplicity, the notion that digital media might provide a remedy for social distance and isolation has been much in vogue since the pandemic hit. At the same time, due to its prefix, the term 're-mediation' underlines the representative character of the phenomena it names, thus neutralizing illusions of transparency and immediacy. Despite seeking the effacement of mediation in their desire to achieve the real, acts of remediation generally involve the multiplication of media, leading to what Bolter and Grusin call the double logic of remediation: a dialectics between immediacy and hypermediacy.[2] In allowing a glimpse of the illusions evoked by digital media, while at the same time providing the key to their unmasking, the concept of 'remediation' proves to be particularly useful in examining the disruption of the senses at the core of the pandemic.

Yet the faith in digital reparation is not the only illusion that the notion of remediation might help us to avoid. At the antipodes of the flawed belief that new media can replicate and substitute for in-person experiences lies the equally deceptive notion that an experience untouched by technology is somehow more 'original' or more 'natural'. In this context, it is the affinity between the notions of 'remediation' and 'supplement', which Derrida developed to undermine the dichotomy between writing and speech, that should be stressed.[3] In fact, it does not follow from a recognition that remediated and in-person experiences, similarly to writing and speech, are of a very different kind that the latter (as presence) takes precedence over the former (as absence). This is what the notion of 're mediation' immediately evinces: it brings to the fore the fact that 'non-remediated' experience is always already 'mediated'. The claim to naturalness or originality of any experience, based on the argument of it being free of artifice, is as flawed as the confusion between in-person and remediated experiences. As will become apparent, the concept of remediation is key to avoiding the misjudgements of both the enthusiasts and the detractors of digital technologies.

In laying the groundwork for what follows, it is crucial not only to underline the accord between the 'remediation of experience' and the 'disruption of the senses' but also to clarify that the latter does not primarily refer to the senses of sight, hearing, touch, smell and taste. The functioning of our sensory system has remained unchanged. It is not a question of thinking, in the manner of McLuhan, in terms of extensions or amputations of the sense organs.[4] The disturbance that our senses have suffered, which affects the scale, pace and pattern of human experience, pertains more to imagination than to perception. That a certain phenomenon is perceived as close or distant in space and time tells us nothing about how it affects us from that proximity or distance. That this same phenomenon can be recognized as more or less threatening, more or less touching, more or less urgent, is something that only the intervention of imagination, which Kant famously called a 'hidden art in the depths of the human soul',[5] can explain. What has changed, due to continual exposure to and dependency on digital remediation, is precisely how this intervention, whereby imagination predetermines the meaning of proximity and distance, takes place. In the digital age, the sense of proximity and distance slips out of its constraints. Fear, agitation, yearning, impatience and hope are all felt differently. Their meaning changes as the material and transcendental conditions of their emergence mutate.

These changes implicate a variety of domains of human life, in particular those whose logic depends for its emotional and intellectual significance on the recognition of distance and proximity. Among these domains are love, study, art, community and travel. In fact, what are all of these if not instances of a dialectic between moving closer and distancing – from the other (love), the unknown (study), the enigmatic (art), the common (community) and the remote (travel)? This list of domains is not meant to be exhaustive or definitive. It is, however, illustrative of important mutations that I am interested in mapping in the fields of ethics, politics and culture.

*

The Digital Pandemic offers a distinctive approach to the Covid-19 crisis, examining its consequences in the light of the broader debate about the digital revolution. Unlike many analyses of the pandemic – including those by Giorgio Agamben, Slavoj Žižek, Bruno Latour and Donatella Di Cesare – my approach is neither apocalyptic nor prophetic.[6] Instead, avoiding the traps of futurology, and rather than fearing or welcoming the impact of the pandemic based on already established philosophical systems, it traces an alternative path, seeking to create a chart for understanding both what the pandemic reveals about the world and how it transforms the conditions of human experience.

Chapter 1, 'The scandal of philosophy in times of catastrophe', begins with a flashback to March 2020. It describes the shock of the pandemic and examines the first philosophical responses to it, notably those of Agamben, Žižek and Byung-Chul Han. In contextualizing their questions, hypotheses and suspicions, I also bring to light how much their analyses draw on pre-existing concerns: about the conditions for political revolution (Žižek), the normalization of the state of exception (Agamben) or the rise of digital surveillance (Han). The logic of fear is also discussed. In times of catastrophe, the task of philosophy consists of not giving in to fear-induced pressure: not only the pressure to find immediate answers to urgent questions but also the pressure to ask the questions that most people, especially in the midst of uncertainty and confusion, want to see answered.

Continuing this line of thought, Chapter 2, 'Questions, hypotheses, suspicions', approaches the pandemic from the standpoint of the dialectic of revelation and transformation. I argue that the crucial question about the pandemic emerges from a certain articulation of the questions about its *transformative* and *revelatory* dimensions. Most authors, from the fields of philosophy to sociology to psychology, have focused either on how the pandemic *transforms* the world or on what the pandemic *reveals* about humanity. While the former approach is common in philosophy (Žižek, Latour, Butler), the latter is omnipresent in humanist approaches, which suggest that the pandemic is also an opportunity for us to rediscover ourselves. Against this backdrop, my claim is that the pandemic reveals more about (the current state of) the world than about (the essence of) humanity and that the transformation of ourselves takes precedence over that of society and culture at large. The pandemic did not change humanity overnight. But it is changing the way we live, feel, desire, think and act. Our forms of life – *how* we are rather than *what* we are – are undergoing a metamorphosis.

In Chapter 3, 'Topology of the imagination', I examine the different ways in which the pandemic has impacted our spatial and temporal experiences in relation to our notions of proximity and distance. When it comes to our experience of space we feel closer to what is distant and more distant to what is close. At the same time, we feel alienated from our past and our future, as if both what happened before the pandemic started and what will happen when it is finally over belonged to a different universe. I explore this diagnosis as an opportunity to recognize the urgency of the present moment. I also establish an analogy between mechanical reproduction and digital remediation. Drawing on Walter Benjamin, I underline that the new technologies of digital remediation express not only a 'promise of proximity' but also an 'equalization of distances'. This leads me to the suggestion that, despite their various dangers and pitfalls, new media deserve more political credit than the detractors of digital technology are willing to concede.

This argument is developed in Chapter 4, 'Apocalypse remediated', which echoes the title of Umberto Eco's 1964 book, *Apocalypse Postponed*. Our current situation, in which the intensified use of digital media is met by apocalyptical fears about the harms of technology, bears similarities to the situation described by Eco. At the same time, his analysis shows that the genealogy of apocalyptical thinking is tinged with elitist and conservative undertones. There is a need to distinguish between political-ecological concerns (the rise of global inequalities, the threats of data mining or the perils of climate change) and ontological-existential preoccupations (the dematerialization of experience, the alienation of consciousness or the loss of presence). Based on this distinction, which suggests that affirming the former does not entail embracing the latter, my point is not to downplay the dangers of digital technologies, but rather to make a strong case for their critical appropriation.

Chapter 5, 'The disruption of the senses', resumes and develops the main argument of the book, namely, that the pandemic has disrupted the way we imagine proximity and distance. It also stresses that, despite the theoretical decision to distinguish between perception and imagination, the two are inevitably bound together. I go on to explore five domains in which this disruption has been felt most acutely: love, travel, study, community and art. In doing so, I consider a variety of topics: from dating apps to meta-photography, to the crisis of the university in the age of digitalization, to the obsolescence of streets as the primary political arenas, to the blurring of the divide between liveness and mediation in the performing arts.

Finally, the Epilogue sheds light on the political implications of the book, bringing together issues of technology, ecology and globalization. The pandemic has been a truly global crisis. In this context, the need to hone a planetary consciousness and sensibility – the promise of which, felt in the wake of the pandemic shock,

has faded away under the weight of routine and exhaustion –
remains crucial. Yet this relies not only on the *abstract* agreement
on political and ecological matters but also on *concrete* experiences
of belonging, care and joy, which are the true matter of love, travel,
study, community and art. Today, these experiences can only unfold
at a global level by means of digital technologies. In a world in which
climate change is accelerating and the threat of authoritarianism is
on the rise, cultivating the power of imagination – not against but
in conjunction with technology – is more urgent than ever.

*

Originally published in Portuguese as *A Torção dos Sentidos:
Pandemia e Remediação Digital* in December 2020, *The Digital
Pandemic* was written in the spring and summer of 2020.[7] Much
has changed since then, and I have updated and expanded the
translated manuscript, so as to reflect these changes. One thing
remains certain: the pandemic will eventually recede. We are now
closer to that moment. Some people hope that life will go back
to normal, but this is also what causes, or should cause, anxiety.
Charting a course between hope and anxiety, this book seeks to
examine the scars of the Covid-19 pandemic as traces of a near
future that has been in evidence for some time. In the face of this
future, into which we have suddenly been catapulted, we must take
a stand. The changes that the pandemic revealed and accelerated
were already underway; they were precipitated by it more than
they were caused by it. The digital revolution is not of today or of
yesterday, and the gradual metamorphosis of the human being that
it implies is inevitable. What is not inevitable is the course that this
metamorphosis will take. We do not have to be people to whom
something just happens. As far as the transformations revealed
and precipitated by this pandemic are concerned, we are as much
subject to the event as we are its subjects.

CHAPTER ONE

The scandal of philosophy in times of catastrophe

1. As time passes, our memories of the beginning of 2020, when the Covid-19 pandemic broke out, are becoming less and less vivid. It is thus worth recalling the widely shared impression of witnessing a totally unexpected event, one that for my generation can only be compared, in terms of the perplexity it caused, with the collapse of the Twin Towers in 2001. The surprise that gripped the world turned swiftly to bewilderment and panic. What had happened? What kind of disaster was this? It was not a natural catastrophe like an earthquake, a tsunami or a meteorite. It was not an act of terrorism. It was not a stock market crash. It was a virus: invisible, like every other virus, but with a speed of propagation and a lethality that would prompt governments to take measures that would previously have been unimaginable. Above all, it was a virus about which worryingly little was known.

Establishing the truth about this new, insidious enemy was paramount. People needed to convert their doubts – the harbinger of fear – into certainty as quickly as possible. They buried themselves in avalanches of calculations, statistics, exponentials, curves, plateaux and peaks. The value of certainty itself – or simply the promise of certainty, the hope of certainty, the mere glimpse of anything that might possibly resemble a certainty – attained its own dizzying peak. The black market in home-made certainties, whether graphics, charts or remedies, boomed. In a time characterized by the hunger for certainty, *a certain distancing* is required from philosophy: a demand that it should not cede to the pressure to obtain answers.

Answers were needed, though, more than ever before: the moment called for medical, logistical and political solutions. Active public scrutiny of policy decisions as they happened was – and remains – necessary. People have denounced, rightly, the necropolitics prepared to sacrifice lives at the altar of economics; they have drawn attention, rightly, to the global dimension of the crisis and the need for international solidarity; and they have condemned, rightly, acts of authoritarianism ushered in by the climate of emergency. All of this was and remains fundamental. But if we do not need philosophy to understand it – and I do not think we do – then the question arises: what role might philosophy play under such circumstances? At a moment that demands the proximity associated with the intervention in the public sphere, how does the distance of philosophy express itself? To what extent is it useful or even, perhaps, necessary?

2. I want to examine some texts by Giorgio Agamben, which generated intense debate early in the pandemic. Before discussing the question he poses, I will consider Agamben's error. This consisted in approaching the problem of the pandemic, which he branded an 'invention', as if he was possessed of *certainty* about its minimal severity.[1] He, a philosopher, did not and does not have the tools to establish the seriousness of the disease. Agamben reformulated his view in a later text, entitled 'Reflections on the Plague', in which he says, 'the following reflections do not concern the epidemic itself but focus instead on what we can glean from human reactions to it'.[2] He goes on to outline the terms of the question I propose to explore:

> They are, in other words, thoughts on how easily an entire society surrendered to the feeling of its being plague-ridden and accepted self-isolation and the suspension of its normal life conditions: its work relations and friendships, its connections to loved ones and to its religious and political beliefs. Why hasn't there been, as would be quite imaginable and as usually occurs in these cases, opposition?[3]

I won't discuss Agamben's hypothesis that the 'plague' already existed, albeit unconsciously, in the form of discomfort with a profoundly misguided way of life, but rather the question he poses, which I consider to be accurate. This might sound perplexing. How is it possible for a question to be accurate, independently of the correctness of its answer and the validity of the hypotheses and suspicions that gave rise to it? This is precisely the claim I want to make to develop some wider points about the role of philosophy in times of catastrophe.

The relevance of some questions lies in their capacity to illuminate the impulse to question itself, not just as 'cause' but also as 'consequence'. This does not so much involve scrutinizing the validity and efficacy of a method, in terms of its capacity to yield a correct answer, as it implies asking questions of the question. What experiences, aspirations, memories, ruses and fears prompt us to ask one question, to privilege that question over another, to answer it in a certain way, or to demand an immediate response to that particular question? Which other questions do we fail to raise when all our attention is focused on obtaining the answer to that single question?

Since March 2020, the question 'how and when will we escape this pandemic?' became hegemonic to the point of making us forget – or even wish to silence – other questions. This is a not insignificant part of the danger we are facing. Agamben's question is accurate because it touches on a sore spot: the risk of blinding ourselves through mono-questioning. It is also accurate because it suggests that the way to deal clear-sightedly with what assaults us is to resist the temptation to put everything – including love, liberty and the courage to ask other questions – on hold to place our trust in the hands of the first entity, institution or discourse that promises an answer or antidote, if not to the virus, then to the fear that the uncertainty around it has generated.

At the heart of the question 'how and when will we escape this pandemic?' the fear of not knowing, of still not knowing, of knowing too late, shouts more loudly than the desire to be given the answer. This was a frightened question, an impatient question, a question quick to grow irritated with anyone who might want to think about other things or ask other questions. At the most basic level, it was a question unable to accept that it still did not have an answer. This is the paradox in which the global *doxa* became mired through its initial response to the pandemic. While it rushed to reject obscurantism and give the floor to science, it also rejected, not without dogmatism, almost with authoritarianism, the idea that science could also be uncertain.

3. Turning to science in the face of a pandemic is the right course of action. However, it is not a simple course of action: science does not speak with one voice, and it does not and cannot provide immediate certainties. It cannot produce a vaccine overnight. It is divided on the best methods for controlling the outbreak. To remember the limitations of science – of which the best scientists are perfectly sentient – is in no way to attack it. On the contrary, in the context of the generalized hysteria that followed the declaration of a pandemic by the World Health Organization on 11 March 2020, to remember the limitations of science was to protect it from the pressure exerted on it by the hunger for certainty. Philosophy can play a role in this context insofar as the questions it poses, which are not to be confused with those posed by science, reclaim for science some important room for manoeuvre.

Today this hunger for certainty is also a symptom. It reflects a defensive reaction to fake news. Fake news provides the best nourishment for negationist opinions about the seriousness of the disease and the importance of vaccination. In the context of the Covid-19 pandemic, fighting fake news is not just a matter of establishing the truth but also of saving lives. In a country like Brazil, disinformation, negationism and necropolitics go hand in hand.[4] But the 'true' is not the symmetrical opposite of the 'false'. The idolization of facts, which some people mistake for a defence of science, is fraught with epistemic and political dangers.

The point is not just that no fact constitutes in and of itself a truth, but also that it is perfectly possible to deceive people without lying. The deceptive effect of fake news goes far beyond the creation of alternative facts. Social media provide numerous examples of this apparent paradox, in which manipulation occurs through the wilful misapprehension and decontextualization of facts rather than their sheer fabrication. In this case, the obsession with factuality creates a smoke screen through which it is hardly possible to spot the difference between the true and the false. Neither science nor philosophy can operate without interpretation, and both are right to reject the misleading equation between the establishment of facts and the clarification of truth. Just as the search for truth does not amount to the enumeration of facts, when it comes to philosophy, the question that one asks, that one *chooses* to ask, is of the utmost importance.

4. There is a need to interrogate the present by not asking the questions the present asks. The questions employed by philosophy to interrogate its own time are not the same as the questions that this time poses or wants to see answered. They can be precisely those it does not want to hear: questions that, more than unpopular, are irritating, if not scandalous. However it is not to *épater les bourgeois*, or for that matter the proletarians or the aristocrats, that philosophy wields its question marks. Its purpose is not merely negative, let alone a matter of irreverence. While philosophy's *questions* are almost always linked to *hypotheses* and *suspicions*, their pertinence – and in this the gap between philosophy and science is a chasm – does not stem from the attempt to expand our knowledge about the real.

According to Karl Marx's famous adage in his 'Theses on Feuerbach', 'philosophers have only *interpreted* the world in various ways; the point is to *change* it'.[5] Theodor W. Adorno alludes to this in his *Negative Dialectic*, suggesting that 'philosophy, which once seemed obsolete, lives on because the moment to realise it was missed', to which he adds that 'the summary judgment that it had merely interpreted the world, that resignation in the face of reality had crippled it in itself, becomes a defeatism of reason after the attempt to change the world miscarried'.[6] This philosophical knot can be untied and retied in various ways, or, as Franco 'Bifo' Berardi suggested a few years ago, chopped off entirely: attempts to transform the world having ended in disaster, Marx's formula should now be inverted and philosophers restricted to interpretation, namely, the task of 'deciphering possibilities' (which are more than just probabilities).[7]

Rather than inverting Marx's formula, I would argue for a reassessment of the relationship between its two mottos: interpretation and transformation. Philosophy can only transform by interpreting and interpret by transforming if it doesn't limit itself to chasing the truth about the real and the possible. The questions, hypotheses and suspicions that philosophy raises do not aim at *that* truth. Instead of seeking compliance with reality, they unfold as non-compliant ideas that stir up reality. In doing so, they are engaged in both interpretation and transformation.

5. To return to the debate about the pandemic, the above applies both to the hypothesis advanced by Slavoj Žižek that the pandemic

represents a fatal blow to global capitalism and to the suspicion nurtured by Byung-Chul Han that increased surveillance and data control could precipitate a shift towards authoritarianism in Western countries. What sets these two perspectives apart is their tone: one is optimistic, the other pessimistic. It is their similarities, however, that I wish to focus on here (I will consider their opposition further in Chapter 2). Žižek illustrates his hypothesis using an evocative image:

> The ongoing spread of the coronavirus epidemic has also triggered a vast epidemic of ideological viruses which were lying dormant in our societies: fake news, paranoiac conspiracy theories, explosions of racism. [...]
>
> But maybe another and much more beneficent ideological virus will spread and hopefully infect us: the virus of thinking of an alternate society, a society beyond nation-state, a society that actualizes itself in the forms of global solidarity and cooperation. [...]
>
> In the final scene of Quentin Tarantino's *Kill Bill: Volume 2*, Beatrix disables the evil Bill and strikes him with the 'Five Point Palm Exploding Heart Technique', the deadliest blow in all of martial arts. The move consists of a combination of five strikes with one's fingertips to five different pressure points on the target's body – after the target walks away and has taken five steps, their heart explodes in their body and they fall to the floor. [...]
>
> My modest opinion is much more radical: the coronavirus epidemic is a kind of 'Five Point Palm Exploding Heart Technique' on the global capitalist system – a signal that we cannot go on the way we have till now, that a radical change is needed.[8]

The details of the scene chosen by Žižek, from the second part of Quentin Tarantino's cinematic diptych *Kill Bill*, are anything but negligible. The image of a strike to the heart of capitalism suggests a stage-by-stage breakdown rather than an immediate overthrow. Žižek is careful enough to stress that 'what makes this attack so fascinating is the time between being hit and the moment of death: I can have a nice conversation as long as I sit calmly, but I am aware throughout it that the moment I start to walk my heart will explode'.[9] The five steps the victim must take before they fall to the floor could be taken at any time, sooner or later. By using this metaphor, Žižek fends off the caricaturization of his hypothesis: he is not announcing the immediate demise of capitalism. The effect that his hypothesis aims for is what needs to be stressed. Interpreting the pandemic as a 'signal that we cannot go on the way we have till now' and that 'a radical change is needed'[10] is in itself a way of contributing to that change. The philosophical hypothesis, in short, aims not for the maximum alignment with reality, but for the maximum tension between interpretative approximation and transformative distancing.

6. The same applies to Byung-Chul Han's reaction to the outbreak. Unlike Žižek, Han expresses a suspicion.[11] By highlighting the possibility that the pandemic could serve in Western countries as a pretext for the implementation of unprecedented security and control measures, of the sort which have become common in Asia, Han aims not just to *realistically* describe the future but also to *preventatively* envision what it could bring. His description has the characteristics of a warning. The object of his suspicion is that which it wishes to prevent; hence his drastic description of the situation:

> The entire infrastructure for digital surveillance has now turned out to be extremely effective in containing the epidemic. [...]
>
> Chinese mobile phone and Internet providers share sensitive customer data with security services and with ministries of health. The State therefore knows where I am, who I am with, what I do, what I look for, what I think about, what I eat, what I buy, where I go. It is possible that in the future the State will also control body temperature, weight, blood sugar level, etc.: a digital biopolitics that accompanies the digital psychopolitics that actively controls people. [...]
>
> Here too, in regards to the pandemic, the future lies in digitalization. In view of the pandemic, perhaps we should redefine even sovereignty. The sovereign is she or he who has data.[12]

It is interesting to note the positioning along contradictory axes of the arguments of Giorgio Agamben, Slavoj Žižek and Byung-Chul Han. Žižek's interpretation contradicts that of Agamben. How can Agamben – according to Žižek's interpretation – call the pandemic an invention by the powers that be, when it has so clearly thrown a spanner in the works of capitalism? Žižek's optimistic hypothesis is that the pandemic has revealed and accentuated the contradictions at capitalism's heart, a heart to which, in his opinion, the pandemic has struck a fatal blow. Han's interpretation contradicts that of Žižek: how can Žižek assume the pandemic could derail capitalism when capitalism is manifestly wasting no time in taking advantage of the crisis? Han's pessimistic hypothesis, in this sense much in the spirit of Naomi Klein's 'shock doctrine', is that an increase in authoritarianism is far more probable (and thus important to resist) than the emergence of some sort of spirit of mutual aid or movement of international solidarity.[13]

Both Žižek and Han employ distancing from a reality they perceive to be negative. I would argue that they use this distancing to look in a similar direction, towards the horizon of a post-capitalist society, a world capable of putting the brakes on what has become its direction of travel, namely, as Isabelle Stengers puts it, a headlong rush from catastrophe to catastrophe, in the direction of the abyss.[14] What distinguishes the two texts are the perspectives they use as their starting points. Žižek introduces the idea of 'the virus of thinking of an alternate society, a society beyond nation-state, a society that actualizes itself in the forms of global solidarity and cooperation'.[15] This is a society towards the realization of which Žižek's hypothesis seeks to contribute. Han, in contrast, proposes that the virus 'is a mirror that reflects back to us the crises in our society'.[16] He presents the reality in which we live, arguing that our current 'burnout society' is moving inexorably towards becoming a 'survival society'. Far from promoting global solidarity, fear of the virus is accentuating individualism. By sketching this vision of a society of isolation, mistrust and exhaustion, Han aims to avert it.

7. The times we are in are times of uncertainty; more than that, of threatening uncertainty. Our world is full of threats: threat (and fear) of the virus that is among us; threat (and fear) of the crisis it has precipitated; threat (and fear) of the powers that could take advantage of our fear and of the weakness that prevents us from overcoming it. In the end, fear insinuates itself even into our attempts to combat it.

It is important to circumvent fear, to prevent it from holding us hostage to the idea that at moments of threat, emergency or catastrophe there is no time to think. Perhaps the greatest danger we face is the danger of ignoring or forgetting that the desire for certainty and security at any price can lead to the stifling of thought, and thus of all that gives meaning to life.

Philosophy distances itself. However, this distancing represents neither a suspension in time nor an evasion in space. It is not caution. It is a quest for the best angle from which to cope with the threats of the day. Philosophy exists as if fear could not do so much. That is its scandal: it distances itself, through its questions, hypotheses and suspicions, as if there was still time to think.

CHAPTER TWO

Questions, hypotheses, suspicions

1. Let me start with two questions about the pandemic. The first is what it *reveals* about us and the reality that surrounds us. The second is how it *transforms* the way we live and the world we inhabit. The combination of possible answers to these two questions determines the various interpretations that have been offered, in either optimistic or pessimistic terms, to account for this crisis. Both of these questions have been ubiquitous to the point of being difficult to avoid. For this reason, the decisive question is a different one: namely, how to formulate these two questions as to what is *revelatory* and *transformative* about the pandemic in a way that weaves them together against the grain of the present.

The hypothesis outlined in this book, that the pandemic precipitates a disruption of the senses that bind us to the world, is a radicalization of the assumption behind the second question: the notion – by no means unanimously held – that there is something profoundly transformative about this crisis. This radicalization relies on insisting on the first question. The focus in that case is more on what the pandemic reveals about the world than on what it reveals about us. That choice of emphasis is an attempt to avoid the impasse of an abstract reflection on the human condition. My suspicion is that, just as there have been automatic and unthinking reactions about the pandemic having transformed the world overnight, there has also been lazy thinking about the unwelcome virus leading to welcome introspection that will bring us closer to who we really are. The church and the university are so crowded with musings on what it is to be human, livened up or not with the theme of 'being-towards-death', that neither God nor the Devil can avoid being bored by them.

In response to the first question, we must acknowledge that the pandemic has *revealed* the inequalities, tensions and contradictions of global capitalism. Not that they were inscrutable before then, but the new circumstances have made them even more apparent. This will allow us to approach the second question, by exploring the hypothesis that the pandemic has radically transformed our ways of life, in a manner that makes ethical, political and ecological sense.

2. Curiously, the pandemic has left the 'philosopher of the event' speechless. That is not to say that Alain Badiou, the author of *Being and Event*, has written nothing on the subject. He did write an article in which he reflected on the circumstances of the outbreak. But after announcing his view that 'the current situation, characterised by a viral pandemic, was not particularly exceptional',[1] he grew at once exasperated and bored, and said virtually nothing more. The tone of his article is that of someone addressing a subject while simultaneously burying it: 'fine, if you insist, I'll say something about this, namely that there isn't much to say'. Here is a philosopher for whom the pandemic, though worsening many of the world's long-existing problems, has not thrown up anything novel, let alone been characterizable as a transformative event.

I am not suggesting that the pandemic should be seen as an event in Badiou's sense – which involves the encounter with something entirely unexpected in the domains of love, art, science or politics, something that unleashes a procedure of truth, concomitant with a transformation of the subject. I am more inclined to agree with Peter Szendy, when he contends, drawing on Foucault's distinction between 'epidemic' and 'endemic', that rather than just another crisis, what we are currently facing is a genuine shift in our nosological and political paradigms, one leading to a situation that could be described as 'panendemic'. 'After becoming pandemic', Szendy observes, 'the epidemic could end up endemic, though still punctuated by epidemic peaks; but the reverse is also true: the endemic plague of healthcare systems under capitalism has exploded into a pandemic crisis'.[2] While Badiou's theoretical disinterest in something that has caused so much practical upheaval might be perplexing, there is something disarming about his honesty. Instead of attempting to fit reality to a theory or to adapt a theory to reality, he simply observes that, in the context of his own philosophical system, the pandemic cannot be seen as having altered the main problems and challenges of our time.

Despite the boredom and impatience that shines through it, Badiou's text is in fact no more surprising than many others, systematic or aphoristic, that have been written about the current crisis. Pedro Duarte notes that in their responses to the pandemic, neither Giorgio Agamben, Jean-Luc Nancy, Slavoj Žižek, Franco 'Bifo' Berardi nor Bruno Latour have deviated much from their usual philosophical instincts.[3] This should not be viewed as a criticism: every thinker construes the events they are testimony to through the prism of the key concepts, fixed ideas and conceptual characters that make up their singular vision. It can even be said that there is an 'elective affinity', driven by adherence or rejection, between certain philosophical figures and certain historical events: Deleuze and May '68, Badiou and the fall of the Berlin Wall, Agamben and the September 11 attacks.

If a certain element of redundancy is to be expected in any concentrated intellectual effort, we might nonetheless find some traditions and theoretical currents better equipped than others for thinking about the pandemic event. In this context, the contributions of authors in the fields of biopolitics and ecological thought – the names of Roberto Esposito and Bruno Latour come to mind – appear to be particularly relevant.[4] The same applies to conceptual hypotheses such as the 'capitalist realism' of Mark Fisher and the 'shock doctrine' of Naomi Klein.[5]

3. Paradoxically, the concept of 'capitalist realism' – the notion that a coherent alternative to capitalism is impossible to imagine, never mind to realize – appears all the more pertinent at the moment when its descriptive value becomes questionable. In other words, the notion portrays the 'pervasive *atmosphere*, conditioning not only the production of culture but also the regulation of work and education, and acting as a kind of invisible barrier constraining thought and action'[6] against the background of which part of our surprise is to be explained. In fact, not since September 11 have we watched the news unfold around us with such incredulity.

A sequence of previously unthinkable events has unfolded: the closing of borders, the scaling-back of industrial production, the cancellation of activities of every kind. All of this has happened in a very short space of time and in every corner of the globe. As Bruno Latour says:

> The first lesson the coronavirus has taught us is also the most astounding: we have actually proven that it is possible, in a few weeks, to put an economic system on hold everywhere in the world and at the same time, a system that we were told it was impossible to slow down or redirect. To every ecologist's argument about changing our ways of life, there was always the opposing argument about the irreversible force of the 'train of progress' that nothing could derail 'because of globalisation', they would say. And yet it is precisely its globalized character that makes this infamous development so fragile, so likely to do the opposite and come to a screeching halt.[7]

The idea of degrowth, described as hopelessly utopian by the ideological machinery of 'capitalist realism', suddenly appears viable. We did wake up one morning to a world in which the brakes had been applied to growth, and the world did not collapse. It is still not easy to imagine a post-capitalist society, but the idea of decelerating or reorienting our globalized economies is no longer more difficult to envisage than the idea of infinite growth.

It is this disruption in the trajectory of global capitalism that has motivated some of the most optimistic reactions to the pandemic, including the hypotheses put forward by Slavoj Žižek and Judith Butler. Both point to an increased sense of solidarity between people, though the arguments they offer differ in political tone. Žižek, more revolutionary, speaks of new types of global solidarity, part of what will deliver the fatal blow to capitalism described above. Butler joins the debate about the future of the US health system. In the wake of the failed presidential campaigns of Bernie Sanders and Elizabeth Warren, she focuses on the way these reignited people's desire for 'a social and economic world in which it is radically unacceptable that some would have access to a vaccine that can save their lives when others should be denied access on the grounds that they cannot pay or could not secure insurance that would pay or because they lacked a visa or legal status'.[8]

Focusing on environmental aspects, Bruno Latour also establishes a nexus between the shock of the pandemic and a beneficial change in consciousness. Comparing the spread of a virus to the spread of an idea, he goes as far as to say that, 'Covid has given us a model of contamination' and that it is an 'incredible demonstration of network theory'. He goes on to argue that 'the big climate questions can make individuals feel small and impotent, but the virus gives us a lesson: if you spread from one mouth to another, you can viralise the world very fast. That knowledge can re-empower us.'[9]

Jordi Carmona Hurtado takes this thinking even further. Pursuing a line of reasoning close to that of Latour, as well as referencing the work of Isabelle Stengers, he suggests that SARS-CoV-2, the enemy currently laying siege to our bodies, could become an ally. He recommends we 'recognise the enemy's virtues … for this event is also a strange kind of ecological ally'.[10] To begin with, the pandemic lends itself to interpretation as an immune response by the entire planet. Markus Gabriel makes the same suggestion; after stating that 'the Earth's ecosystem might still turn out to be one giant living organism', he asks: 'is the coronavirus a planetary immune response against human hubris leading to the destruction of countless creatures simply out of greed for profit?'[11] For Hurtado, however, the pandemic is also a warning: humanity's final chance, perhaps, to take a different direction:

> The shock therapy of the pandemic is achieving something no ecological campaign has ever achieved: that we finally enter the dynamic of degrowth that is necessary to halt our headlong rush towards collapse. The happy effects of this degrowth are beginning to be felt around us: birds are singing again in the hearts of cities where before we heard only the grunting of cars, skies eternally darkened by factory fumes have cleared, the water of rivers and canals is clean again, wild boars walk down deserted roads. The carnival of non-human life is slowly returning.[12]

4. One thinker who has not waxed lyrical about the viralization of good ideas or the carnival of life is Naomi Klein. For the author of *Shock Doctrine*, the pandemic could well lead to significant changes in the ways our societies are organized, but it is highly doubtful that these changes will be for the better. In an article focusing on New York State, Klein points out that the lids were barely closed on the

coffins of the first Covid victims when those eager to transform the catastrophe into a business opportunity began to meet. The New York State governor, Andrew Cuomo, announced the involvement of the Bill and Melinda Gates Foundation, as well as Google's former CEO, Eric Schmidt, in a newly formed commission to reimagine the state post-pandemic. Klein argues that companies such as Google, Apple and Amazon are using the crisis to advance their agendas and assert their interests. For her, the pandemic may have revealed something about the fragility of capitalism, but not as much as it has revealed about its predatory agility, resilience and mutability. The future suggested by the 'Screen New Deal' will involve major changes in areas such as education and health, and it does not look bright:

> This is a future in which, for the privileged, almost everything is home delivered, either virtually via streaming and cloud technology, or physically via driverless vehicle or drone, then screen 'shared' on a mediated platform. It's a future that employs far fewer teachers, doctors, and drivers. It accepts no cash or credit cards (under guise of virus control) and has skeletal mass transit and far less live art. It's a future that claims to be run on 'artificial intelligence' but is actually held together by tens of millions of anonymous workers tucked away in warehouses, data centers, content moderation mills, electronic sweatshops, lithium mines, industrial farms, meat-processing plants, and prisons, where they are left unprotected from disease and hyperexploitation. It's a future in which our every move, our every word, our every relationship is trackable, traceable, and data-mineable by unprecedented collaborations between government and tech giants.[13]

Our response, Klein suggests, should not be to reject technology, but to demand the democratization of decision-making about its use. This would entail a decisive intervention in the public space to denounce the abuses by governments and corporations and to trigger critical thinking in a society that has been stunned into inaction by the pandemic shock. Klein's ideas are in this sense compatible with those of thinkers who identify a link between the pandemic shock and the emergence of a new global political and environmental consciousness. However, according to Klein, this consciousness cannot be developed without fighting against the numbness created by the general shock.

There is another sense in which pandemic optimism has tended to trip up on its own enthusiasm: it has fostered the assumption that the viralization of good ideas, occurring more and more at a global level, translates into genuine and lasting adherence to them. The pandemic has been unprecedented in the way it has transported us to the global plane. Neither last century's world wars nor previous financial crises have been global to this extent. Even wider reaching than the fall of the Twin Towers – the consequences of which became global, even though the initial focus was geographically circumscribed – Covid-19 has been the first trauma to be experienced by humanity in every part of the planet simultaneously. People suddenly found themselves worrying about how things were in other parts of the world: the virus that was separating us locally was bringing us closer globally. We had the impression – and this is what the optimistic perspectives predicted and privileged – that a new global awareness flourished in individual sensibilities. While it is important to acknowledge the globality of the crisis, it is also important to unpick the meaning of that globality and to understand how we have positioned ourselves towards it, both intellectually and emotionally.

To use one of the most popular metaphors of the months after the outbreak, while we are all facing the same storm, we are not all in the same boat – or if we are, we are on different decks, and it is not hard to predict what will happen if the boat sinks and there are not enough life jackets onboard. According to David Harvey, 'the progress of COVID-19 exhibits all the characteristics of a class, gendered, and racialized pandemic'.[14] The catastrophe has not been experienced with equal severity in rich countries and poor countries; it does not affect privileged and disadvantaged populations in the same way; it does not have the same repercussions on the lives of men and of women; it does not cause the same disruption to daily routine for someone who lives in a suburb and works in a city centre as for someone who can do their job from home. The 'catastrophe' of the empty toilet paper shelf in the supermarket is a tasteless joke when set against the lack of clean drinking water that affects more regions of the world than those in rich countries like to believe.

In *Immunodemocracy: Capitalistic Asphyxia*, Donatella Di Cesare explores the link between the disease in itself, the fact that Covid-19 compromises respiratory function, and its broader, symbolic meaning. 'Perhaps it is no accident', she claims, 'that the virus proliferated in the respiratory tracts, through which the breath of life passes'.[15] The 'virus of asphyxia' lays bare the ills of our epoch. It shows that 'in this era of advanced capitalism, no one can escape the dizzying economy of time … the growth imperative, the compulsion to produce and the obsession with productivity combine to ensure that freedom and coercion end up coinciding'.[16] In the same vein, Achille Mbembe advances the idea of a 'universal right to breath'. While conceiving of breathing beyond its purely biological aspect, Mbembe weaves together the pandemic, as a humanitarian disaster that affects the world unequally, with the social and ecological threats that predate it.

> Before this virus, humanity was already threatened with suffocation. If war there must be, it cannot so much be against a specific virus as against everything that condemns the majority of humankind to a premature cessation of breathing, everything that fundamentally attacks the respiratory tract, everything that, in the long reign of capitalism, has constrained entire segments of the world population, entire races, to a difficult, panting breath and life of oppression.[17]

For Mbembe, Covid-19 reflects and epitomizes the many pathologies of our globalized world, all that threatens the rhythmic balance between inhalation and exhalation that constitutes human life, both figuratively and literally: from everything that condemns people to a life of oppression, fear or misery to the diseases that may soon result from the aggravation of climate change. For 'at the rate that life on Earth is going, and given what remains of the wealth of the planet, how far away are we really from the time when there will be more carbon dioxide than oxygen to breathe?'[18] Approaching the crisis from a similar angle, Peter Sloterdijk claims that 'the coronavirus pandemic is an emergency strongly hinting that the co-immunism imperative has arrived', for 'one can already see that there is no real private property of immunity advantages'.[19] We cannot understand what this pandemic means without recognizing that, the moment its global reach became apparent, it revealed the deep inequalities that blight our planet. The issue, for those of us enjoying privileged lives in rich countries and being well aware of that fact, is not just that we are not in the same boat. The issue is that the enhancement of global sensibility that causes us to be affected by the situation in other parts of the planet only persists when we feel vulnerable ourselves. When the initial shock recedes, our altruistic sentiments dissolve. The knowledge that our world is unequal does not disappear, but our usual detachment from it returns. In this sense, the pandemic reveals not just the inequalities and contradictions of the world but also the obstacles to the awakening, in our thoughts, feelings and imaginations, of a true global consciousness.

5. Far apart on many issues, Rancière and Badiou coincide in their rejection of pandemic optimism. Rancière expresses scepticism about viewing the pandemic as a 'good opportunity' to challenge capitalism.[20] Badiou goes even further and declares that 'we will also need to pass through a stringent critique every perspective according to which phenomena like epidemics can work *by themselves* in the direction of something that is politically innovative'.[21] Both are right in stressing that the only vehicle for political transformation is human action.

Since the criticisms made by Rancière and Badiou are aimed implicitly at some of the authors referred to above, it should be noted that neither Žižek nor Latour believes that a transformation of reality will occur through the agency of a virus. They both submit to the idea that a transformation of reality could only occur as the result of a change in how reality is perceived and understood. It is because the pandemic reveals the contradictions of the world – the failure of capitalism, the ecological destruction of the planet, the precariousness of political, social and economic equilibria all over the globe – that it could, if that awareness led to action, result in transformation.

The 'pandemic optimism' of Žižek and Latour, as it expressed itself in the first texts they wrote about the outbreak, falls down not because they overlook the dialectic between the subjective consciousness of reality and its objective transformation. Their stressing that good ideas can 'turn viral' bears witness to this. It falls down because of the naivety of their understanding of this 'viral dialectic'. They imagine a contagion of good ideas that is more effective and lasting than seems probable. In addition, they disregard or downplay the fact that the pandemic is already transforming the way we live. Any discussion about possible and desirable contamination by good ideas needs to take this transformation into account.

The imagination – all the ideas by which we envisage the necessary, the probable and the possible – presides over the transformation of the world. Yet it is precisely the imagination, of all human faculties, that is suffering the greatest shock. The more pessimistic analyses of Donatella Di Cesare and Byung-Chul Han, with their emphasis on the impact of digital technologies on our consciousness, prove themselves necessary. It is not a question of giving in to pessimism, but of finding a non-naive optimism, one that recognizes that the measures taken to contain the pandemic are already transforming our ways of life.

6. There is despair in the air. We fear the contamination of our bodies, but our ways of life are also threatened by obsolescence. The concrete transformations that might result from the pandemic are inseparable from transformations in the ways we think, feel and act. That is why allowing the discussion on what is revelatory about the pandemic to become a reflection on the human condition will not serve us. To take that route would amount to suggesting that the pandemic, along with the feelings of isolation and vulnerability caused by it, prompts us to grasp our essence: to examine our relation to time, our dependency on others, our relationship with mortality. It would be as if humanity – or, to be more precise, the minority of humans able to indulge in such luxuries – had entered a meditative retreat. The pandemic, to quote one shepherd of souls, would then provide 'an opportunity to rediscover ourselves'.[22]

Certainly, some reflections on the human condition, namely those that explore the nature of community, are politically committed. From this perspective, they do not differ from the approaches to the pandemic taken by Žižek or Mbembe. This is true of the reflections of Jean-Luc Nancy, for whom the virus 'puts us on a basis of equality, bringing us together in the need to make a common stand', and can help us to 'better understand the nature of our community',[23] and of Tomás Maia, who argues that the pandemic has revealed both our mortal condition and the privatization of the communal aspects of our lives, from the air we breathe to the health care we require, exposing the 'ethical and sanitary failure of an economic and financial system – capitalism – that can only see health, even health, as a commodity, a private *salvation* in all senses of the word'.[24]

The problem with these approaches is that their evocation of the sense of community that the recognition of our common mortal condition implies, while strengthening their political arguments on the normative plane, weaken them on the descriptive plane. Roberto Esposito's insight that in modernity the experience of *community* is inseparable from the exigency of *immunity* became vividly apparent as the pandemic began to unfold.[25] Even though neither the shepherd of souls nor the promoter of ideals might be willing to recognize it, the glue of our modern community – which the state, as defined by Hobbes in the seventeenth century, has been mandated by the masses of the twenty-first century to produce without interruption – is a belief in immunity to the other. Peter Sloterdijk goes even further in envisioning history as a battle of immune systems.[26] Yet, according to him, the pandemic has changed the meaning of that battle. 'From now on', Sloterdijk argues, 'protectionism of the whole is the directive of what I call "immunitary reason"'.[27]

We are also, as Paul B. Preciado points out, 'in the throes of the transition from a written to a cyber-oral society, from an industrial to an immaterial economy'.[28] In José Gil's terms, the pandemic has become a 'mediating agent' between two types of society and subjectivity, accelerating the 'passage from one historical phase of capitalism (industrial/financial capitalism) … to another phase in which we make necessary adjustments between economic demands and the subjectivities that can respond to them, in fields from home working to leisure pursuits'.[29] It is through this process that new forms of subjectivity arise.

The politicization of the debate on the existential, psychological and ethical consequences of the pandemic is crucial. In pursuing it, we should not ignore the transformations that impact the human condition, but fight from the position inside the storm they have produced. Instead of rejecting ethics in the name of politics, we must recognize that the ethics of the *Homo digitalis* needs to be politicized. To advocate a return to an idealized 'more organic' or 'less virtual' pre-digital revolution way of life is as absurd today as it was in Marx's time to advocate a return to an idealized 'more natural' or 'less alienated' pre-Industrial Revolution way of life. Paul B. Preciado outlines the challenge that faces us:

Just as the virus mutates, if we want to resist submission, we must also mutate. We must go from a forced mutation to a chosen mutation. We must operate a critical reappropriation of biopolitical techniques and their pharmacopornographic devices. First, it is imperative to modify the relationship between our bodies and biovigilant machines of biocontrol: They are not only communication devices. We must learn collectively to alter them.[30]

7. According to the Institute of Health Metrics (at the time of writing in July 2021), the Covid-19 pandemic may have caused nearly 10 million deaths worldwide, more than double the number officially recorded (4.5 million). The death toll is likely to surpass 15 million in 2022.[31] These figures and projections are inarguably worrying. However, they should be viewed in the context of other figures. We don't need to go back a century, when the Spanish flu killed about 50 million people just after the First World War: in 2019, according to the World Health Organization, 52 million people died as a result of poverty or diseases caused by poverty.

Why mention these numbers? Certainly not to minimize the severity of Covid-19, but to make a simple point: if the pandemic has shaken the world, this is not because of the lethality of the virus, but because of its capacity to spread, our perception of the threat it poses and the consequences of the measures that have been taken to contain it. If, for some unfathomable reason, SARS-CoV-2, or a much more lethal virus, had not reached the richest, most privileged and most developed countries of the world, and even if fatalities were far higher, we would be talking in terms of unpleasant news rather than of catastrophe. Only by understanding this will we be able to approach the questions as to what is *revelatory* and *transformative* about the pandemic in an 'untimely' manner.

The pandemic does not just reveal the inequalities in our world but also the extent to which we have normalized these inequalities. It shows both the need to and the difficulty of achieving a global consciousness. Moreover, considering that the measures in place have neither prevented the deaths nor held economic and social upheaval at bay, the pandemic also revealed the instability of the foundations on which global capitalism has built its over-ambitious scheme. Everything is interconnected: people, markets, information, ideas and affections. This interconnectedness, fundamental to the logic of capitalism, turns out to be its weak spot.

The pandemic has revealed all of this, but as we scrabble to draw theoretical conclusions or formulate practical plans, it carries on transforming our lives. We feel disoriented: the instruments we formerly used to calibrate the ordinary and the exceptional are no longer reliable. Our understanding of distance and proximity has been scrambled in a way that is unprecedented in the history of humanity, this being the first global catastrophe of the digital age. The pandemic is not the event. The event, before any revolution or involution to come, is the resulting transformation of our modes of existence – a transformation taking the form of a disruption of the senses that bind us to the world.

This hypothesis may be less hyperbolic than it first appears. The virus has neither altered humanity nor revealed its essence. It has not led to the collapse of capitalism. It has neither rescued nor condemned the planet. But the way we understand and situate ourselves in the world has experienced a shock of the sort we have not seen for a long time. The pandemic has not changed *what* we are but *how* we are. The ways in which we live, think, desire, imagine and act are all undergoing a metamorphosis. In the face of this metamorphosis, and right in the midst of it, we must take a position.

CHAPTER THREE

Topology of the imagination

1. It has become commonplace to imagine the Covid-19 pandemic as having shaken the foundations of global civilization. Slavoj Žižek's 2020 book, *Pandemic!: COVID-19 Shakes the World*, is an obvious example, but similar metaphors are used by Byung-Chul Han. For a society, he claims, in which an excess of positivity and an increase of digitalization prevail, the emergence of a 'real virus' – as distinct from a 'computer virus' – amounts to the traumatic return of the real in all of its negativity and resistance. 'Here it is a real virus, and not a computer virus, that causes a shock. The real, and therefore resistance, is again noticeable in the form of an enemy virus.'[1] It is this real, Han suggests, that suddenly afflicted humans and the planet. Metaphorically speaking, it is as though the pandemic caused a planetary earthquake followed by a mass concussion.

The comparison of the impact of the pandemic with a bodily injury strikes me as evocative. I would like to further explore it, albeit in a different direction. During the periods of global quarantine, however isolated people were, they continued to communicate, interact, love, work and study. But they had to change the way they did all of these things. Reorganizing bodily rhythms and mental routines, they began to fix their eyes more often on screens, hunch their shoulders more often over computers, smartphones and tablets. The injury caused by the pandemic resulted from both the unexpected shock of reality and the sudden need to adjust the posture of the body. The emergency demanded swift adaptation. As well as a concussion, the pandemic produced a crick in the neck.

At first glance, we might conceive of this injury as a painful contraction caused by an abrupt transition between acceleration and braking. A little further down the line, however, it might be imagined more as an adjustment leading to a rearranging of faculties, perhaps even to new forms of mental flexibility. When the compass is broken, the north of proximity and the south of distance are replaced with a disconcerting floating in space and time. We feel disoriented. Every place needs to be reimagined.

2. Today, and increasingly since the pandemic first shook the planet and our bodies, we are forced to envision the digital revolution along the same lines as Karl Marx viewed the Industrial Revolution – as the source of that 'general illumination which bathes all the other colours and modifies their particularity'.[2] Herbert Blau, quoting this very passage from Marx, claims that cinema – which became possible due to the emergence of the mechanical reproduction of sound and image – was the 'ether' of the twentieth century.[3] Similarly, we might state that the 'ether' of our early twenty-first century is the digital remediation of audiovisual experiences that renders the representation of reality more malleable than ever. It is this ether, to return to Marx's terms, that 'determines the specific gravity of every being which has materialized within it'.[4] Everything is subject to its influence, inebriated on it.

This inebriation can give rise to numerous anxieties, and these have been made more acute by the confinement at home and the exile from society demanded by quarantine. What kind of life are we living? Are the classes on Zoom, the concerts on YouTube and the conversations on WhatsApp really classes, concerts and conversations, or are they impoverished, adulterated or inauthentic simulacra of teaching, learning, artistic practice, aesthetic experience and human interaction?

There is a tendency to mistrust distance, but we should avoid the fallacy of equating the use of technologies that allow for distanced contact with an acceptance, let alone a defence, of distancing. It is nonsensical to curse these technologies as much as or even more than we curse the virus itself. By making distanced socializing, learning and fruition possible, new media do aim for proximity: they provide what could be termed a 'promise of proximity'.

Whilst we should scrutinize the exact nature of that proximity, and ask who is profiting by promising it and whether the promise can be kept, we must recognize this promise as a salient feature of the new media. For better or worse, digital remediation is the heir to the technical reproduction that revolutionized the modern experience in the transition between the nineteenth and twentieth centuries.

3. In his reflections on the impact of technology on art and politics, Walter Benjamin emphasized the political implications of this 'promise of proximity'. This is particularly apparent in his famous – albeit not always well-understood – essay 'The Work of Art in the Age of its Technological Reproducibility'. The positive aspect of technical reproduction is precisely its ability to bring things, specifically works of art, closer to people. Benjamin interprets this phenomenon in terms of its social basis and identifies two circumstances behind it, 'namely, the desire of the present-day masses to "get closer" to things, and their equally passionate concern for overcoming each thing's uniqueness by assimilating it as a reproduction'.[5] This 'desire to get closer to things' is the key to grasping the political importance of cinema, photography and all other artistic practices that make use of the possibility of technical reproduction offered by the modern era.

In light of this, the result of technical reproduction, by which 'each thing's uniqueness' is overcome, is the transformation of visible or audible verticality into tactile horizontality. Such is the sensory translation of its political meaning. The original painting of the *Mona Lisa* in the Louvre can only be viewed from a certain distance, but a photographic reproduction of it can be touched, cut or juxtaposed in a collage with any other image. A sound recording can be manipulated, interrupted or restarted later. Nothing is so distant, inaccessible or elevated that it cannot be brought closer to people through technological reproducibility. This principle is dynamite to the hierarchies that govern the experiencing and creation of art and the places where art and life intersect.

This bringing closer concerns both visual and auditory objects, whose existence expands in space and time. In fact, distance in time can be reduced just as effectively as distance in space. The telephone can bring the voice of someone far away closer. Phonography, preserving the auditory present, and photography, preserving the visual present, are footprints that can be followed by those who will come in the future to get closer to what occurred in the past. We are so accustomed to these records that we often forget their potency. They bear witness to long-past events and long-dead people that are fading from the memories of the living. Take, for instance, the diffidence on the face of the Newhaven fishwife photographed by David Octavius Hill and Robert Adamson in the mid-nineteenth century, or the vocal aplomb of Gustave Eiffel, recorded by phonograph in 1891 at the top of the tower that bears his name.[6] These records continue to transform themselves with every second that passes. They become traces of a past that is more and more distant, beckoning to us from further and further away.

According to Benjamin, the technological transformations at the turn of the nineteenth and twentieth centuries generate a kaleidoscopic horizontality that causes the collapse of hierarchies: not only between the sacred and the profane, the extraordinary and the uneventful, the sublime and the vulgar, but also between the ephemeral and the permanent, what is lost of the past and what is conserved for the future. The price of this bringing closer is the relinquishing of the experience of something unique and unrepeatable – Benjamin's much-quoted 'decay of the aura'. While looking at a photograph or listening to a recording, one is offered a version of that which is reproduced that implies a renouncing of the original. One must be content with a copy, a copy that lacks what only the original provides: the authenticity of a here-and-now encounter with a unique occurrence or object. This lack generates a mistrust that has never completely disappeared and which resurfaces today in the form of anxiety about the remediated experience.

4. We take fright, like the narrator of *In Search of Lost Time*, when, on the phone to his grandmother, he has a premonition of her imminent death. Her voice sounds close, but it is a spectral, disembodied voice that is about to disintegrate in time, 'a phantom as impalpable as the one that would perhaps come back to visit me when my grandmother was dead'.[7] He rushes to his grandmother's house. At the door to the living room, he sees her absorbed in a book, and is frightened all over again: in the moment before she becomes aware of his presence, she appears to him as she would in a photograph. The phantom is back.

Just as the Proustian narrator seeks physical proximity to his grandmother to confirm to himself that she is alive, we crave experiences that are unequivocally real to confirm that we ourselves are real. It would be vain to ignore the differences between live and remediated experience or to downplay the losses inherent in a shift from one to the other. As we gain the capacity to bridge spatial distance by technological means – the phone calls of a century ago are no different from the video calls of today – we lose what co-presence alone is able to ignite: a multisensory experience that involves not only visual and auditory stimulation but also the senses of touch, smell and taste. In the experiences of love and travel, as well as in every aspect of life or art predicated on the touching or intertwining of bodies, the losses are immense. The logic of power, the dynamics of seduction and the impact of silencing are also disrupted.

Benjamin, whose observations remain relevant if we accept the analogy between mechanical reproduction and digital remediation, provides us with a touchstone for deepening this debate. The dialectic of gains and losses does not amount to an opposition between advantages and disadvantages. Some losses, he intimates, can be seen as advantages. This is precisely what is at stake in the 'decay of the aura'. The loss in this case goes hand in hand with an increase in familiarity with the work of art and an expansion of its possible uses; it also represents a blow, as John Berger would put it, to the mystification of art.[8] Curiously, the fact that this idea – that sometimes the *loss* of authenticity involves a *gain* in familiarity and accessibility – may also apply to our current situation is something that not even scholars of Benjamin have so far been able to admit, let alone been keen to investigate.

While recognizing that the (human) 'proximity' made possible by technical reproduction is distinct from the (spatial) 'proximity' afforded by co-presence, Benjamin points out that co-presence has its own forms of distancing. The protocols involved in visiting a museum, and the means of guaranteeing physical and imaginary distance between visitors and artworks, are the heirs to the paradigmatic experience of distanced co-presence that is the veneration of cult objects in a religious building. In other words, there are modes of spatial proximity that actively encourage human distance and the creation of hierarchies in relationships between people and between people and objects, symbols and institutions. It is these forms of distancing – grounded in concepts such as 'respect' and 'authority' – that technological reproduction renders obsolete or inoperable, and it is in this sense that the loss of authenticity can be an advantage, when these forms of distancing and hierarchization collapse along with it.

The forms of proximity that were made possible by technological reproducibility – and are also fostered by digital remediation – enhance the 'Sinn für das Gleichartige in der Welt' (sense of all that is the same in the world). This has political implications, not the least because 'Gleichartige' (all that is the same) contains the suggestion of 'Gleichheit' (equality). A century ago, Benjamin contrasted the cinema actor with the theatre actor, observing that the former relinquishes some of their power over their audience because the camera they must remain trapped behind disarms them of their charisma. Today, we might make a similar comparison between teaching at a distance and teaching in a physical classroom. In the latter case, the teacher can take in the whole of the student body with a single glance, can get up, move closer or further away, and can represent themselves, as an actor represents their character, to command the respect of an audience that is, for its part, required to remain immobile. The digitally remediated teacher is in front of a computer screen in a physical position identical to that of the students. If invited to intervene, the students do so under the same audiovisual circumstances as the teacher. By virtue of everyone using a digital device, the meeting resembles one between equals.

Another element of Benjamin's concept of the 'sense of all that is the same/equal' has particular relevance in the pandemic context. Digital remediation, while deepening and expanding the effects of mechanical reproduction, not only allows a bringing closer by shortening human distance and circumventing spatial distance but also abolishes the frontier between the accessible and the inaccessible: as well as a 'promise of proximity', digital remediation offers an 'equalization of distances'. In today's world, more than ever before, the sensation that all distances are equal becomes hegemonic.

This awareness was intensified by the specific circumstances of quarantine: when physical distance was imposed on people, the Proustian narrator inside them could not go to their grandmother's house. Yet the inevitability of this distance gave rise to a feeling that all distant things, irrespective of how distant they were, were *equally* susceptible to being brought closer. The friend who had moved to another part of the country was now no further away than the friend in the same neighbourhood; a conference on another continent could now be attended as easily as one at the local university; the decision about whether to see a performance in Chicago, Lisbon or Tokyo was now one of time zone rather than geographical distance.

5. Although the measures taken to contain the spread of the virus principally affected people's relationship with space, their relationship with time also suffered a shock. The restrictions precluded walks, trips, visits, excursions and meetings – that is, everything that happens outside the home. Yet the isolation and immobility have also generated what Peter Szendy calls 'an internal polyphony in which different temporalities and speeds are superimposed'.[9]

The pandemic prompted both braking and acceleration. While some people had to stay inside, others, including health workers, postal workers and couriers, were required to go out: the demobilization of the rest of society intensified their mobilization. The feeling of simultaneous braking and acceleration was experienced at an individual level too. Alongside the slowing of the rhythm of leaving and returning to the house came a virtual rush to reorganize work, education, shopping, socializing and leisure. People remained deployable and available, to paraphrase Maurizio Ferraris[10] and Hartmut Rosa.[11] The quarantine did not stop the activity and commotion of daily life. In fact, in some cases, it even intensified it by limiting it to the domestic environment. But the background was one of interruption, much like the movement of a wheel that keeps spinning after a vehicle has skidded and flipped over. People gazed in awe at this wheel that was the world still turning around and inside them – yet moving nowhere.

By showing that acceleration and braking are not incompatible, the pandemic is not without consequences to the debate on accelerationism.[12] Whether one favours the claim that acceleration can be an antidote to capitalism (as accelerationist theorists postulate) or embrace the counterargument that speed will only enhance capitalism's destructive tendencies (as its critics maintain), we have to admit that 'capitalist acceleration' and 'technological acceleration' do not immediately coincide. It is undeniable that capitalism exploits technology for its own ends, but it also clear – and the pandemic made it even clearer – that their soft spots are distinct. While the world halted, its 'nervous system', the digital infrastructure of communication, on which our lives are more and more dependent, moved faster.

However temporary and fragile, this paradox between 'economic slowing down' and 'technological speeding up' bears important consequences. It lends plausibility to the suggestion that it is possible to counteract capitalism, as Benjamin Noys recommends, with 'a sense of friction that interrupts and disrupts the fundamental accelerationist fantasy of smooth integration',[13] without abandoning the conviction, expressed by Alex Williams and Nick Srnicek, that the 'recovery of lost possible futures, and indeed the recovery of the future as such'[14] will not be possible without technology, or, to be more precise, without reimagining its uses and ends. The idea that this requires us to 'accelerate the process of technological evolution',[15] as the authors of the *Manifesto for an Accelerationist Politics* claim, is open to discussion and criticism, yet the notion that the conjunction of technophobia, nostalgia and localism weakens anti-capitalist struggles remains indisputable. As Benjamin Noys himself observes, 'a return to the human, or a simple decelerative equilibrium, withdrawal, or new ascetism'[16] will not do.

Beyond the dialectic between braking and acceleration, the pandemic offered an opportunity to other mental experiences. The circumstances of the 2020 global quarantine embodied an interruption, which was perhaps not the interval of a night of deep sleep, into which, as Jonathan Crary notes, 'glimpses of an unlived life, of a postponed life, can edge faintly into awareness',[17] but still that of a midday nap from which one awakes with a sense of disorientation first and then of newfound alertness. Confined at home, some people became more attentive to the things around them – the objects they kept, displayed and used; that served them, sheltered them and looked at them.

Emanuele Coccia suggests that 'if there will be a revolution it will be a domestic revolution', adding that it will imply a new understanding of the house 'as a place where things come alive and make life possible for us'.[18] This is not a matter of fetishism – an attachment to commodities whose 'use value' is always already determined by their 'exchange value' – but of a special kind of animism. Domestic objects speak to us and of us. They speak to us about experiences and feelings we once had. But in so doing they remind us of our past and future selves, inasmuch as those memories of the past inevitably include projects, plans and dreams for the future. Isolated at home, stuck in space, people began to adventure in time, not so much explorers of subjectivity as distracted *flâneurs* in the palimpsest of the events and episodes that formed their own lives.

6. With a view to characterizing the pandemic's impact on our relationship with space, I mentioned a 'getting closer to the distant' and a 'becoming equal of distances'. Social isolation and digital remediation, while preventing people from (physically) approaching what was *close*, allowed them to reach out to what was (geographically) *distant*. They began to imagine and feel distances as equivalent. The love for the distant (foreigner) and the love for the close (neighbour) became confused. The hope of a global consciousness sprang up. What about our relationship with time? One important difference must be noted from the outset. Unlike the 'here', that provides the epicentre for all and any distance in space, the 'now' that localizes us in time is at once an ending point for the past and a starting point for the future. What we understand as close or distant in time has two distinct meanings, depending on whether we approach it from the perspective of the time that has passed or the time that is to come. Bringing the distance of the past closer is like following a trail: excavating ruins, deciphering palimpsests, studying archives. Bringing the distance of the future closer is an exercise in prediction, a weaving together of longing and fear, utopia and dystopia.

The interruption of the pandemic event seems to have precipitated an equalization of distances with regard to both past and future. In the case of the past, recent memories and early memories began to seem equally distant. 'A few months ago' and 'many years ago' both seemed to apply to a life irremediably lost. The same happened with the future: so many plans had to be deferred that the idea of a fully fledged resumption of life – rather than the resorting to a new normal – felt like a mirage. 'In a few months' and 'in many years' seemed equally uncertain. The technologies of remediation confirmed and reinforced these impressions: they allowed for a glimpse – whether nostalgic or hopeful – of what was and what will be. Perhaps for the first time, we looked at photographs and videos on social media with nostalgia, when previously they seemed like records of an eternal present. Perhaps for the first time, we regarded future plans, the realization of which always seemed imminent, as desirable but uncertain. In her first Norton Lecture ('Spending the War Without You: The River'), delivered on 10 February 2021, Laurie Anderson describes precisely this feeling.

> Time these days can seem mirage-like. You are walking along towards the future and out there, all these things in the distance: people, projects and places. And you keep walking towards them but instead of getting bigger and closer these things keep getting smaller, farther and farther away as they get cancelled, rescheduled, cancelled again – finally, just erased. And it becomes an act of faith to keep going forward.[19]

All of this suggests that the distance separating us from the past and the future has grown deeper. The equalization of distances that, in the case of our relationship with space, went hand in hand with a promise of proximity became, in the case of our relationship with time, a recognition of distance: 'yesterday' and 'tomorrow' appeared as far away as 'once in the past' and 'at some point in the future'. If, in terms of the 'here', we felt closer to other places, people and experiences, and were catapulted to a global scale, in terms of the 'now', we experienced the distance of the past and the future alike as a symptom of the urgency of the present. We were precipitated into the present instant, and into the sensation that this was the moment in which we could change our lives.

7. The passage in which Walter Benjamin distinguishes between the concepts of 'trace' and 'aura' is well known:

> The trace [*Spur*] is the appearance of a closeness [*Erscheinung einer Nähe*], however distant whatever left it behind might be. The aura [*Aura*] is the appearance of a distance [*Erscheinung einer Ferne*], however close whatever calls it forth might be. The trace makes the thing possessible by us; the aura takes possession of us.[20]

The difficulty of interpreting this passage stems from the way it oscillates between understanding the relationship between 'closeness' and 'distance' as something we perceive and as something we imagine. When he uses the expressions 'however distant' (*so fern das sein mag*) and 'however close' (*so nah das sein mag*), Benjamin is referring to the perception of objects in space and time. When he refers to the appearance of a closeness (*Nähe*) in the trace and of a distance (*Ferne*) in the aura, however, he shifts from the plane of perception to the plane of imagination. His point is that, just as the trace allows us to gain possession of something distant (such as prey that is in fact distant in space but that has left tracks which allow us to imagine it to be close), the aura allows something close (such as an artwork that is in fact close in space but the aura of which causes us to imagine it to be distant) to take possession of us.

The dialectic between trace and aura is a key narrative for our times. The challenge is to catch hold of the trace without succumbing to the aura, to hunt without being hunted, to reach without being reached, to capture without being captured. In today's world, however, what permits us to take possession of the distant, by following the traces of a distant knowledge, feeling or desire, also permits the distance – a new distance, with an unknown face, but a pull and an influence we sense – to take possession of us. The internet and social networks permit us to search for experience, content and encounters. We embrace the proximity of the far away and the equalization of distances. But with every step we take, the swamp of zeros and ones we traverse is registering our trajectory. When we follow traces, we leave traces. Those traces, of the places we go, the merchandise we acquire, the goods we consume, the services we contract and the tastes we show, all combine to form a *single* profile of who we are. We have a face. We are recognizable. We feel exposed.

In following traces, we expose ourselves to traps. Yet let us not be paralyzed by caution. Let us not allow ourselves to be captured, even by the fear of being captured. We need to move forwards in stealthy, elusive and agile ways. If the pandemic event has shifted the imagined places of the close and the distant in space and in time, through the power of the technologies that allow us to reach and be reached, seek and be sought, capture and be captured, then the challenge is one of capture and escape, a dance between truth and fiction, a game of disguise and metamorphosis.

CHAPTER FOUR

Apocalypse remediated

1. For the apocalyptic intellectual, these are catastrophic times. The pandemic is yet another sign of humanity's sleepwalk towards the abyss. Barbarism and obscurantism are on the increase, inequality is growing, time is running out to prevent ecological disaster. We are complicit in our own alienation; we detach ourselves from the world, binge on entertainment, make ourselves available, mobilizable and exploitable. We imagine everything except the logical conclusion of the behaviour that is pushing us towards the precipice; we indulge and collaborate with our oppressor and our gatekeeper; we welcome the digital revolution with blindness and naivety. In a word, we have relinquished who we are and allowed ourselves to be captured by the forces that threaten us. In apocalyptic thinking, there is a tendency to conflate concerns about human alienation – 'we've relinquished who we are' – with those about the dangers of the digital revolution – 'we've allowed ourselves to be captured'. My aim here is to investigate what separates them. It is only by doing this that we will be able to reject this brand of catastrophism without succumbing to the complacency and naivety it rightly denounces.

2. The title of this chapter might prompt a sense of déjà vu. It is intended to evoke the Italian philosopher Umberto Eco's 1964 work *Apocalypse Postponed*, in which he distinguishes two contrasting views of mass culture.[1] The holder of the first view, whom Eco calls the 'apocalyptic intellectual', complains of the vulgarization of culture, the superficiality of taste and the alienation of the masses,

evils which have arisen from the increasing hegemony of television, advertising and consumerism. The 'integrated intellectual', on the other hand, sees in the new mass media opportunities for the dissemination of content and for enhanced communication between cultural agents, the public and consumers. The integrated intellectual celebrates innovation and dismisses the concerns of its critics. This polemic remains alive and well, and the pandemic has made it even more bitter. The apocalyptic intellectual has never had so many reasons to complain about the alienation that the integrated intellectual appears to dismiss.

Life has not been easy for apocalyptic intellectuals. In the 1960s, it was still possible for them to roam broadly the same terrain as integrated intellectuals, remaining on the margins, avoiding alienating routes to integration and privileging certain experiences, products or lifestyles over others. Today, the pockets of air in which they could breathe freely are swiftly disappearing. In the context of quarantine, this scarcity – of air, movement and life – has been almost literal. Even the most sober and coherent of the apocalyptic intellectuals has baulked at the inexorability of the remediated experience: refusing it, in such circumstances, being akin to condemning oneself to deafness, muteness and solitude.

Remediation might be imagined as a kind of upgrade, a version 2.0 as it were, of integration. Today, the integrated intellectual is doubly remediated: in the sense that their experience is transposed to digital media and in the sense that these digital media appear to offer the only possible remedy to distance. This sense of inevitability reinforces the impression that remediation and integration are inevitably intertwined: people cannot fail to be integrated if their words, their gestures, their very lives, are remediated. They can battle, as the apocalyptic intellectual does, against integration; they can take issue with the way it instrumentalizes remediation; they can attempt to avoid it. But they cannot pull themselves up by the hair. They cannot keep pressing forwards as if the ground on which they are trying to practise their escapology is not mined, or is not a boggy marshland shrouded in the vapours of the ether of remediation. The voice of the apocalyptic intellectual still sounds discordant. However remediation is now the tuning fork against which it is dissonant; the spirit level according to which it is uneven; the fabric that its colour taints.

The reason I turn to the conceptual characters of the 'apocalyptic' and the 'integrated' intellectual should be teased out. My point is not simply that apocalyptic intellectuals, because they are unable to escape remediation, cannot avoid remaining integrated. According to Eco, by remaining secluded in their ivory towers, observing the grimaces on the faces of the public with detachment, they are complicit in the integration they criticize. Not only do they console themselves with the delusion of the distanced superman, they also contradict themselves by using the tools of mass communication to express their opposition. Eco quips, 'integration, thrown out of the door, comes back through the window'.[2] Needless to say, the same applies to the apocalyptic intellectuals of today, on whose Facebook and Twitter pages texts by Giorgio Agamben and Byung-Chul Han are posted, commented on and shared.

This argument, which is relatively self-evident and not particularly shrewd, is not the one I am interested in exploring further here. Instead I evoke Eco's distinction between the apocalyptic and the integrated intellectual because it provides me with a touchstone for two other interrelated investigations that illuminate and support one another. The first is to sketch a genealogy of the apocalyptic attitude, with the aim of charting the role played in it by the critique of technology (decisive if we wish to grasp the ambivalence of today's critiques of digital technologies). The second is to argue for the need, in our current context, for a double negation of the extreme attitudes of the apocalyptic and the integrated intellectual (the categorical detractor and the credulous enthusiast of the new media). Insofar as it draws on this genealogy, this double negation amounts to the conviction that, as far as attitudes to technology are concerned, a rejection of the lenience and naivety of the integrated intellectual must not give way to the conservatism and elitism of the apocalyptic intellectual.

3. It is indisputable that digital technologies are new instruments in the service of integration, manipulation and exploitation. It comes as no surprise, then, that the apocalyptic intellectual, with a keen eye on the twin dangers of cultural alienation and political authoritarianism, has turned their attention away from the culture industry at the heart of mass culture and towards the digital revolution.

It should be noted that the distrust of technology of the apocalyptic intellectual did not emerge in the 1960s – the golden era of the critique of 'culture industry' – let alone today. In his genealogy of the apocalyptic attitude, Eco reminds us that, from the time of the debates between Marx and Bauer, distrust of technology – in particular of mass reproduction technology – has frequently gone hand in hand with elitism, an insistence on the gulf between popular massification and critical erudition, and even a Manichean distinction between the lucidity of the reflective intellectual and the stupidity of the masses. In this regard, Eco anticipates many of Rancière's ideas about equality and emancipation. Not unlike Eco, Rancière suggests that the strategies employed to emancipate allegedly ignorant or alienated people, whether proletarians or spectators, are often of a sort that continually reproduces the inequality they aim to overcome.[3] Today, this commonality between the two authors is obscured by the fact that Eco eagerly participated the postmodern debate, while Rancière fundamentally dismisses its terms and validity.[4]

Of particular importance in Eco's argument is his suggestion that, while the critiques of integration are necessary, we cannot subscribe to them wholesale. It is not a question of denying that integration should be approached with lucidity and a critical spirit. Eco does not shy away from declaring that 'the function of the apocalyptic intellectual has a special validity – that of denouncing the optimistic ideology of the integrated intellectuals as profoundly false and in bad faith'.[5] It is rather that we must find ways of framing this critique that do not create dubious distinctions between authenticity and alienation – assuming introspection to guarantee the first and technology to encourage the second – or between the thinking of the intellectual and that of the wider population – assuming careful deliberation and distinctive clarity from the first and a chaotic brew of reactions, desires and opinions from the second.

Hence the importance of our double negation of the attitudes of the integrated and apocalyptic intellectuals: the challenge is to recognize the dangers of integration without succumbing to the reactionary impulses that can insinuate themselves, often almost imperceptibly, into apocalyptic discourse. Only by doing this can we address the political and ideological anxieties the digital revolution provokes – all that the apocalyptic thinker is right to criticize about integration – without ourselves joining the chorus lamenting the alienation of the human condition or the oblivion of an originary connection to the world engendered by technology.

4. Over the last few decades, Bernard Stiegler, Paul Virilio, Shoshana Zuboff, Maurizio Ferraris, Byung-Chul Han and Roberto Simanowski have all devoted increasing energy to exploring the dangers of the digital revolution. Their themes, distinct but overlapping, include the rise of entropy from the spirit of computational capitalism, the compulsion to accelerate and its consequences for human perception, the commodification of human experience as behavioural data and prediction products, the self-mobilization of the subject, the transformation of biopolitics into psychopolitics, and the threats of data mining and algorithmic regulation.[6]

We need to recognize not just the importance of these studies but the breadth of their focus. I referred above to the fact that the critique of the massification of culture has transformed into a critique of the digitalization of culture. It can now be added that today's apocalyptic intellectuals do not restrict themselves to culture; they also explore ethical, social, economic, political and ecological fields. True, the critique of mass culture was never just a critique of what is strictly defined as culture: the forms of reification it objected to arose from a symbiosis of culture, politics and economics. Today, however, our reference point is Zygmunt Bauman rather than György Lukács: the objection is to a liquefaction, rather than a reification, of experience.[7] The target of today's apocalyptic critic is not just cultural alienation, but the condition of permanent connection, exposure, availability, mobilization and exploitation in which we find ourselves. As long as we continue to be swept along by these currents, we are unable to focus on the increasing deterioration of democratic institutions or the imminent ecological catastrophe. In fact, it is with regard to ecological matters that the apocalyptic discourse is not only legitimate but also, as Latour argues, urgently necessary.[8]

That said, and while stressing the seriousness of the ecological crisis and threat of surveillance capitalism, a point should be noted that is not always adequately highlighted in contemporary ecological-political discourse, namely that digital technology has a decisive role to play in the shrinking of humanity's ecological footprint. It is not possible to conceive of a radical transformation of the conditions of human dwelling and mobility in the context of dynamics of degrowth without the strategic use of digital technologies – unless we renounce the prospect of a global consciousness and awareness. Similarly, a regeneration of democratic life is hardly conceivable in isolation from digital media. It is crucial not to equate technology with the uses it is put to by companies such as Google, Facebook or Microsoft. Data mining is not inscribed in the DNA of digital technologies. As Shoshana Zuboff stresses, we need to challenge the claims of technological inevitability and recognize that 'surveillance capitalism is not technology; it is a logic that imbues technology and commands it into action. Surveillance capitalism is a market form that is unimaginable outside the digital milieu, but it is not the same as the "digital".'[9]

Digital media are not just instigators of apathy, frustration or isolation (as is the case when social networks determine intersubjectivity) or instruments of manipulation, surveillance and control (as is the case when companies, parties and political powers get access to big data). We should refrain from concluding that 'surveillance capitalism', 'data capitalism'[10] or 'computational capitalism'[11] will necessarily have the last word on how digital technologies affect human experience on an individual and social level. Depending on the uses to which they are put, these media can also be opportunities for intellectual emancipation and the broadening of cultural horizons. I am not referring to immediately available information, which is often incomplete, imprecise or incorrect, but to the vast heritage of scientific, literary and artistic knowledge that today is just a download away. Thanks to collaborative peer-to-peer networks and file sharing, today's internet gives global access to what the Library of Alexandria used to provide at a local level: a potentially universal archive in which anybody can find anything, from a critical edition of Ovid's *Metamorphoses* to the latest album by Protomartyr. The availability of information does not of course guarantee the generation of knowledge, but numerous functionalities of digital media, from editing and search features to hyperlink functions, can also be said to facilitate learning and appropriation.

The recognition of these potential advantages does not resolve the problems diagnosed by Bernard Stiegler, Shoshana Zuboff or Roberto Simanowski. In any critical examination of the digital revolution, however, it is essential to scrutinize the complexity of the phenomena, to be aware that technology is not isolated from society and economy, and to attempt to avoid the insinuation of the anxious little voice whimpering that 'we've relinquished who we are!'.

5. Critical reflections about digital surveillance, data control or the manipulation of algorithms can give way with surprising ease to ontological and existential anxieties of a conservative slant. In his book *In the Swarm*, Byung-Chul Han references one of Kafka's letters, in which the writer deplores the fact that a letter allows a distant person to be thought about, but not hugged or kissed. This, says Kafka, transforms them into a kind of ghost. Byung-Chul Han comments:

> Since then, Kafka's ghosts have also invented the Internet, smartphones, email, Twitter, Facebook, and Google Glass. Kafka would say that the new generation of ghosts – digital ghosts – are more gluttonous, more shameless, and noisier than ever. Isn't it a fact that digital media reach 'beyond human power'? Aren't they leading to a racing, uncontrollable proliferation of ghosts? Are we not, in truth, losing the ability to think of someone far away and hold on to someone nearby?[12]

At the outbreak of the pandemic, Giorgio Agamben similarly spoke of the 'erasure of every sensory experience and the loss of the gaze, which is now lastingly imprisoned in a spectral screen'[13] and foresaw that 'wherever possible digital devices will replace any contact – any contagion – between human beings'.[14] In the same vein, Donatella Di Cesare warned that 'the face-to-face based on physical proximity to the other ... has given way to a situation in which our senses are denied contact with our peers' and that '"social distance" confines the – infected, infectious, infectable – body and consigns it to an aseptic, sterile virtuality', thus concluding that 'the digital medium interposes itself, separating even as it allows communication'.[15]

These descriptions of 'racing, uncontrollable proliferation of ghosts', 'erasure of every sensory experience' and 'aseptic, sterile virtuality' suggest that a malign genie has captured the bodies and spirits of humanity. By conflating political and ecological concerns with existential and ontological anxieties, the apocalyptic thinker can allow their critical contribution to be buried under a mountain of fears: of the dematerialization of experience, the virtualization of relationships, the spectralization of the other, the loss of the organic, the blunting of the senses, the disconnection from the world and the indifference to the earth.

6. Three observations suggest themselves at this point. The first relates to the somewhat imprecise use of the terms 'virtual' and 'spectral'. Digital technologies do convert images, sounds and texts into numbers, thus rendering them independent of any material support. As Friedrich H. Kittler puts it, 'inside the computers themselves everything becomes a number: quantity without image, sound, or voice'.[16] In this sense, we can indeed speak of dematerialization. However the dematerialization of the *contents* of the experience does not necessarily imply a dematerialization of the *experience* of the contents. It is of the order of superstition to suggest that the sound resulting from the reproduction of an MP3 file is less concrete or more virtual and spectral than that produced by the reproduction of a CD or a vinyl record.[17] The same applies to the listening experience they provide.

The second and third observations concern respectively the *place* that remediation occupies amongst our experiences and the *type* of experience it comprises in itself. To begin with the obvious: the screen of a computer or a smartphone is not more or less material than the surface of a mirror or a pane of glass. When we use these artefacts, we interact with them through our eyes, ears and fingers. While perceiving the contents they remediate, we also continue to see, hear and feel the objects and people around us. Digital media may affect the human capacity to concentrate. Video games may become addictive and social networks may create disinterest in face-to-face social experiences, but the effects of these technologies cannot be seriously understood or discussed without reference to the educational, social and cultural contexts of their use. Technological remediation occupies *one* place amongst our perceptive and imaginative experiences; it does not take *the* place of all of them. This held true even during the isolation of global quarantine: while technologies of remediation might have imposed themselves on people's daily lives with unprecedented intensity and frequency, many of these people also found their attention to the domestic sphere equally heightened.

To come to the third observation, we should be clear about what type of experience remediation *is not*. The remediation of experience – or, to be more precise, the remediated experience of a specific reality or object – *is not* the substitution of that experience. It doesn't aim to be a cure for a lack. The ills of physical distance, bodily absence and psychic isolation have no remedy. It is *another* experience of the *same* reality, and one that is overtly incomplete because, as a rule, it only reproduces the visual and auditory components of the remediated reality. When we attend a performance online or communicate by video call, we see and hear but do not smell, touch or taste. We *see* text that we read and images we look at, *hear* music or spoken words we listen to, *see* and *hear* a news report or a concert.

A technology capable of restoring the five senses simultaneously is imaginable, however. *Strange Days*, the science-fiction film directed by Kathryn Bigelow in 1995, which serves as a touchstone for Bolter and Grusin at the beginning of their book *Remediation: Understanding New Media*, is based on this premise.[18] The technology around which the film centres allows for the recording of any multisensory experience: to replay the recording of that experience is to see, hear, smell, touch and taste it just as the person whose experience was recorded saw, heard, smelled, touched and tasted it. Interestingly, though, even the radical example of this film does not present the remediated experience as capable of substituting a complete experience. Even if it were possible to record and reproduce a multisensory experience, we would still be talking of an experience that someone else had in the past. It would still lack the spontaneity and unpredictability of a first-person experience in the here and now.

Jumping from 1995 to 2018, the first episode of the fifth series of *Black Mirror*, 'Striking Vipers', takes this speculation further by combining it with the notion of virtual reality. It imagines a new version of a combat simulator game that allows the player to *enter* the virtual reality and embody a fighter. The simulator reproduces the sensation of pain of every blow, and, being an upgrade of the original game in more than one sense, is also able to reproduce the sensation of sexual pleasure. As in *Strange Days*, the remediation of the sexual act is a key aspect of the plot, but the difference in 'Striking Vipers' is that the remediation is not of a sexual experience had by another person in the past, but of one had by the player of the game themselves in the present moment. The player can control their movements in the game and feel the effects of those movements in the here and now, although this 'here and now' happens in a virtual world, while their actual body remains still, prone on a sofa, as if asleep. Does this fiction represent a total remediation of experience, in which there is complete substitution of a real experience for a virtual one?

The answer would seem to be yes, but only up to a point: there is a decisive element in the narrative of this episode that persuades me to make that qualification. The story revolves around a heterosexual couple, Danny and Theo, and their single friend, Karl. The two players in the game are the two men, Danny and Karl, long-term friends, who the narrative has suggested are both heterosexual. Assuming the bodies of a man called Lance and a woman called Roxette, they become sexually involved in the virtual world. Later they discuss whether they might have been hiding their homosexuality from themselves up until now. To test this, they kiss. Neither feels anything. The excitement that overtook them in the virtual world has no corollary in the real world. While the pleasure they experienced in the artificial paradises of the game really existed, its realization in the virtual world did not correspond to the satisfaction of a desire they had repressed in the real world. In the final analysis, we cannot speak of remediation as a remedy in this case either, not because the experience of the virtual bodies is less real than that of the physical bodies, but because the virtual reality was not used to compensate for a pre-existing lack.

7. In facing the challenges of the present, apocalyptic critics tend to rely on an intellectual crutch. Whether explicitly or not, they assume that it is possible to abstract the human condition from the historical contingencies of technological development. It is in accordance with this assumption, and by means of the contrasts it allows them to draw, that they conduct their analysis and fight their battles. The question thus arises as to whether we need to take up arms against the digital revolution in defence of the materiality, concreteness and authenticity of human experience. The conclusion I reach in this text sits in opposition to apocalyptic reason by contesting that the fight against technology is at once unjustified, hopeless and misdirected.

It is unjustified because it is rooted in a reductive and partial conception of the role of technology in human history. It is important to view the digital revolution, as we should view all scientific progress and technological developments, with a critical eye. The alliance between technology and capitalism should also be exposed and scrutinized. However, this critical spirit should not be confused with nostalgia and technophobia nor pander to an elitist and conservative brand of humanism. Beyond this, even if such a fight were fully justified, it would be doomed to failure from the start: when it comes to the human condition, the die is cast, and its rolling is inseparable from technological evolution. As Bernard Stiegler notes in his trilogy *Technics and Time*, 'humanity and technics are indissociable'.[19] While the combative stance of the apocalyptic intellectuals is right, their target is wrong. What will serve us best is not a generic rejection of digital technology, but a keener understanding of its uses, potential, illusions, dangers and threats.

Digital technology is more than just a tool for the forces of capitalism. It does not foster only individualism. It is not limited to simulating proximity. It can also create community links and emancipatory opportunities for flight and capture. It can collapse distances and hierarchies. Saying so does not reduce the worry engendered by a recognition of its dangers. However, it invites us to accept the challenge of shaping a force that is in the process of transformation instead of waving in the air – like placards inscribed with watchwords or commandments – dichotomies between 'digital' and 'analogue', 'material' and 'immaterial', 'concrete' and 'spectral' or, finally, 'technics' and 'civilization'. As Bernard Stiegler writes, 'those who oppose technics to civilization do not accept that, as the versions of the Prometheus/Epimetheus myth in Hesiod, Aeschylus, and Protagoras teach us, humans are prosthetic beings, without qualities, and that temporality … emanates from this de-fault of and at the origin, this originary disorientation', and he continues:

They do not accept it precisely because in fact it is sometimes quite difficult to accept, and because one's skin must be sufficiently thick to do so. But, just as important, they do not accept the idea because this fundamental disorientation is at its most extreme limit today: our contemporary experience of it is unique, nearly unbearable, and requires *very* thick skin indeed – and yet strangely, in our current circumstances it is equally important to have very sensitive, indeed *hyper*sensitive skin, and perhaps even ... *to completely change our skin.*[20]

In today's world, no one can escape being both apocalyptic *and* remediated. Our situation is more complex than that described by Eco. The pandemic has pushed us into a paradoxical position, in which the apocalyptic thinker *in us* cannot escape (the condition of) remediation, and the remediated thinker *in us* cannot escape (the prospect of) apocalypse. While remediation filters the way we imagine our existence in the world, it is impossible for us to ignore our apocalyptic anxieties. The fight is immanent. It is our own skin that is at stake.

CHAPTER FIVE

The disruption of the senses

Gradually, without our awareness, the pandemic and the measures taken to contain it have transformed our lives. I am not referring to the use of masks, or the restrictions on mobility, or even the anxiety provoked by the waves of contagion or the spread of new variants. These are mere epiphenomena. For the event reaches far deeper, leaving us dazed and wondering what has happened – as if, to remember Nietzsche, we have tried to 'count all the twelve reverberating strokes of our experience, of our life, of our being – oh! and lost count'.[1] The pandemic has shaken the foundations on which the imagination of the distant and the close rests, thus stirring up the sense of everything we know, wish for and are capable of. This stirring up is what I call the disruption of the senses. In other words, the event consists of the growing impact that the combination of social distancing and exacerbated use of digital technologies is having on the senses that situate us in the world.

In this chapter, I will explore five of the areas of human life in which this disruption is most acutely felt: love, travel, study, community and art. It might seem a random selection, something akin to the taxonomy of animals collected by Jorge Luis Borges in a certain Chinese encyclopaedia, the 'wonderment' of which Foucault recalls at the beginning of *The Order of Things*.[2] By grouping them together, I do not mean to suggest that these domains are the only sources of meaning in human existence. The reason for this selection lies in the fact that however diverse our experiences of them may be, love, travel, study, community and art are all predicated on a recognition of what is close and what is distant. Moreover, in terms both of *what* they mean for us and *how* they mean for us, all can be described as exercises in bringing closer and distancing.

What is travel if not the experience of traversing distances in space to spend time in proximity with other customs and ways of life? What is love if not the elusive 'good distance' that fuels attraction? Could study not be defined as bringing oneself closer to what one does not yet know, conquering the territory of ignorance, or as discovering unexpected proximities, recognizing affinities and developing connections? Community, for its part, is inconceivable without the construction of the imagined bonds that bring us closer to each other. Finally, art can be seen as an exercise in tackling and elaborating the enigmatic, namely a getting closer to the uninterpretable, the irreconcilable and the unassimilable.

To diagnose the disruption of the senses is not possible without redrawing the parallels and meridians of the distant and the close that the shock of the pandemic has displaced. Nor is it possible without recognizing the new forms of distance and proximity that the digital revolution has made either viable or obsolete, or without taking the pulse of the new experiences of solitude, empathy, escape, forgetfulness, pleasure, fatigue and habitation that have emerged with it. It is not just a case of making a diagnosis, however; we must also assume a position, both towards the event and towards the anxieties it induces. Hence the importance of the distinction, outlined in the previous chapter, between the political-ecological preoccupations and the ontological-existential concerns that manifest themselves in contemporary apocalyptic discourse. Only through a clear-sighted exploration of this distinction, unfolding it on a case-by-case basis, can we avoid apocalyptic catastrophism – and the elitism, conservatism and technophobia it often leads to – without falling into the traps of naivety and conformity.

The event has manifested itself in love, travel, study, community and art very differently. The reason for this is that the essential meaning of distance and proximity at stake in these domains varies as we move from a literal register (as when we consider travel) to a metaphorical one (as when we consider study). Therefore, the strategies I will adopt to discuss each of these domains will also be distinct, comprising the deconstruction of false problems, the identification of risks, the exploration of possibilities, the dismantling of traps and fugitive planning. What follows, to conclude, resembles a labyrinth of notes more than an ordered path. Its aim is not to cover the fields approached in an exhaustive manner, but to suggest some tentative and open-ended avenues for reflection.

Love

In the two most commonly observed scenarios, the pandemic has either distanced lovers or brought them closer. Those who did not live together (or decided not to live together during quarantine) were distanced, while those who did live together (or decided to live together during quarantine) were brought closer. In the first scenario, reclusion made it difficult or impossible for people to meet; in the second, uninterrupted cohabitation was required. Jokes did the rounds about the second scenario, predicting either new arrivals nine months later or divorces as soon as quarantine ended. In any case, lockdown was imagined and experienced as a challenge for lovers, whether they found themselves separated or brought together: that of managing either excessive distance or excessive proximity. In this sense, the pandemic reminded us that love itself is an 'art of good distance'. I would like to suggest that it also allowed us to realize that the 'rules' of that art are not defined *a priori*.

Many understood the challenge to lovers presented by the pandemic as a test of love, to be passed by overcoming the excess of either proximity or distance: only true love could withstand uninterrupted cohabitation or enforced separation. This view has a faintly moralistic simplicity. It presupposes that lovers already know, or should already know, what love is, as if it were not, as Rimbaud puts it, a case of constantly reinventing it. Perhaps what the pandemic has in fact cast light on is that need for reinvention. It may be a test for love as much for lovers, the challenge for lovers being not one of proving their love but of reimagining their language.

*

There is no love that is not felt in the body, that can subsist without the real or imagined presence of bodies, that allows either the conscious or the unconscious imagination to dispense with corporeality. For this reason, amongst all the domains of experience under discussion here, love is the one most compromised by physical distance. Distance prevents contact between bodies and the perception and pleasure of touch. But this is not all there is to love, and highlighting this aspect is saying very little about its language. Moreover, it does not account for the fact that proximity, without the balancing presence of its opposite, can be as harmful as distance. Love, through its seduction rites of sex, companionship, sharing, listening, trust and planning, is a dance made up of sorties of moving closer and distancing, all of which presuppose, but also transcend, corporeality.

Whether together (side by side, face to face or intertwined) or apart (separated by walls, streets or borders) lovers are always in search of the good distance: the distance that is vertigo rather than equilibrium, tension rather than compatibility, risk rather than comfort. This art of good distance is the sense of love; nothing to do with common sense or good sense, and never confused with sensible conjugal management. By showing that love is the art of calibrating proximity and distance, and by challenging lovers to reinvent it, the pandemic has the potential to launch a new conversation about conjugal life and about one of its most rarely explored aspects: cohabitation.

Curiously, when discussing the cohabitation of lovers, neither the liberal nor the conservative commentator tends to actually discuss it. Both presuppose it, awarding it more or less legitimacy according to whether the lovers are married or not. The assumption is that cohabitation is the natural destiny for lovers. There is in fact nothing 'natural' about the cohabitation of lovers, just as there is nothing natural about marriage, whether religious or civic, or about a particular sexual orientation, or about the coinciding of sex and gender. The point made by Paul B. Preciado, when he says 'the dildo is not the phallus and does not represent the phallus',[3] could also apply to the house: its use in the context of amorous practices is not determined *a priori*. Both are technologies, and for neither is it possible to assign a 'natural use' aligned with the symbolic function of the 'phallus' or the 'household'.

Lovers in the time of Corona for whom forced cohabitation has been alienating or imposed distance been frustrating have not betrayed their love, as the moralists would have it. On the contrary, they have grappled with the challenges of perseverance and renewal, in the context of which the supposed naturalness of cohabitation is revealed as contingent. This contingency shows that the value of cohabitation for lovers is determined by the context of each individual relationship: it is not a model that lovers should *either* adopt *or* reject *a priori*. We can count it as a positive effect if the experience of forced distance or proximity leads to a growth in this awareness that cohabitation is not a given, but one element of the art of good distance that is love.

Human beings have an incredible capacity to devise ideals. We use them to strengthen and improve ourselves to the point of risking becoming enslaved to them. Yet we also have an incredible capacity to question these ideals. As swiftly as we conjure them, we can pick them up and set them spinning, like the tops in Christopher Nolan's film *Inception* (2010). We watch them as they spin, noting with surprise that they keep their momentum. We need to take hold of them gently and smile at them as we place them down one by one.

*

In a world of social distancing and isolation, the existence of dating apps, such as Tinder, Meetic or OkCupid, seems to entail a contradiction. While allowing strangers to get in touch with each other, the purpose of Tinder is to facilitate their meeting in person. Therefore, despite being a digital app, in which the users interact at a distance, its ultimate purpose – the dating itself – has also been inhibited by the recurrence of quarantines and curfews.

It is ironic, in this context, that the critics of the *dematerialization* of human relations are the same ones who lament the *materialistic* trivialization of romantic encounters. 'What is striking', we read in *Philosophy & Philosophers*, 'is the connection with consumption. Scrolling through profiles (geographically close to you) as you would through the fridges or sofas. ... This trivialization is probably a reflection of a generation that has stopped believing in love. Tinder is the Ikea of dating.'[4] It cannot be ignored that dating apps, by allowing space for disrespectful and dismissive behaviours, frequently leave their users frustrated. But this is not exclusive to online dating. Contrary to what those who complain about the lack *and* the excess of corporeality might think, the threat of dating apps is to be found elsewhere.

In *Praise of Love*, Alain Badiou argues for the necessity not only of reinventing love but also of defending it, namely from a safety-obsessed mentality according to which love could thrive without the experiences of falling or of taking a gamble. To illustrate this idea, he turns to a number of slogans used by the app Meetic, the wording of which has caught his attention:

> 'Get love without chance!' And then another says: 'Be in love without falling in love!' No raptures, right? Then: 'Get perfect love without suffering!' And all thanks to the Meetic dating-site … that offers into the bargain – and the notion takes my breath away – 'coaching in love'. … I believe this hype reflects a safety-first concept of 'love'. It is love comprehensively insured against all risks … Clearly, inasmuch as love is a pleasure almost everyone is looking for, the thing that gives meaning and intensity to almost everyone's life, I am convinced that love cannot be a gift given on the basis of a complete lack of risk.[5]

Badiou's observations touch a nerve. The threat of dating apps lies in neither the dematerialization nor the trivialization of love; rather, it lies in the attempt to calculate the encounter: in the submission of love to the logic of probability and prediction. Conversely, their appeal – the promise that they may or may not fulfil – consists of providing the opportunity to meet someone outside one's bubble. In this light, Facebook, not Tinder, in that it grows from and expands one's pre-existing social and professional circles, would be a more conspicuous menace to love.

*

Eyes cannot meet over Skype. This is made impossible by the fact that the position of the camera, representing the external gaze, does not correspond with that of the eyes of the interlocutor. When one person is looking directly at the other, they do not seem to the other as if they are looking. They can only seem that way if they look directly at the camera, which means taking their eyes off the other. For Byung-Chul Han, the divergence of gaze that characterizes video calling on software such as Skype bears witness to the fact that 'the digital medium is taking us farther and farther away from the *other*'.[6] Only co-presence can allow for symmetry of gaze, meaning that only co-presence can allow for real contact with the other and the reality of love: there is no such thing as a 'virtual relationship'.

Yet there is no such thing as a 'sexual relationship' either. As Lacan wrote, the pleasure of lovers isolates them. During the sexual act, fantasy separates what sexual pleasure appears to unite. Not even when co-presence is unequivocal, when the proximity of bodies is at its most immediate and intense, is this 'relationship' consummated. Drawing a parallel between the 'virtual non-relationship' and the 'sexual non-relationship' invites us to recognize the role of the imagination in every drawing together or apart of lovers, on both physical and spiritual planes.

We are not condemned to solitude. Put simply, whether at the maximum distance or the maximum proximity, no relationship between lovers can exist without imagination. Co-presence is not enough. Not even love – the fire of which is ignited, burns and consumes itself in the vessel of corporeality – has co-presence, whereby eyes meet and bodies touch, as a sufficient condition for consummation. Not even love escapes the realm of the imagination; it may in fact be the domain of human life that escapes from it the least.

Travel

Deleuze distrusted travel. He expressed this opinion during a well-known interview with Claire Parnet, included in the eight-hour television programme 'Gilles Deleuze's alphabet book' (1988–9). He enumerated his reasons for this mistrust, which included that travel could not be a real rupture and that it would, as Beckett put it, be foolish to travel for pleasure. For his final reason, he quoted Proust's observation that people in fact only travel to check whether something they imagine to be the case actually is. In this view, travel betrays difference; it is a delusive rupture characterized by false distractions and false discoveries. Is that really the case? I sense hesitation in Deleuze's voice when he refers, at the end of his observations, to his wanderings in Beirut. I prefer to remain undecided, to take the risk that the promise of difference offered by the experience of travel as a whole might sometimes be deceptive, but perhaps not every time.

*

Travelling is knowing the world by coming into contact with it; getting close to distance and dwelling in it. The experience of travel, like that of love, is multi-sensory: not just sight and hearing, but also taste, smell and touch are involved. It is perhaps during travel, with the movement of our bodies that it demands, that the conjunction of our five senses is employed in its most dynamic way.

Today travel is under threat: the pandemic has made it something to distrust. The virus can travel too, by hitching a ride with people who travel. The circulation of humans around the planet has become a problem. During quarantine, it became impossible, or at least ill-advised, to travel. Airports, ports and stations closed. The almost universal instruction from governments was 'stay at home'. Cities emptied out, their visual and sonic landscapes altered. During lockdown, both tourists and inhabitants disappeared from the streets of Lisbon, Paris and Venice. Tourism was threatened too, but the threat to travel and the threat to tourism should not be confused.

Travel was already under threat before the pandemic, precisely because of tourism. That tourism – along with gentrification – should be a threat to the local inhabitant is fairly self-evident. Perhaps less self-evident is that it is also a threat to the traveller. Yet the traveller is in fact the first victim of tourism. It is never easy to achieve a real rupture through a journey, but the whole purpose of tourism is to make this *a priori* impossible. Tourism impoverishes the traveller, prevents them from stepping out, from taking risks, from meandering. The rupture, for the tourist, is just a mirage. They are no longer even required to set foot in an agency, but simply to click – and an algorithm performs its magic. To use a popular marketing phrase, the aim of tourism is to provide a 'home away from home'.

The tourist and the traveller cannot and should not be confused: if we fail to distinguish between the deception offered to the tourist and the experimentation sought by the traveller, our recognition of the significance of travel will be trampled beneath our critique of tourism. A critique of tourism that fails to safeguard the significance of travel is an invitation to a sedentary life and an apologia for localism, a retreat into our own small country, city and life. And there is no country, city or life, however big or small, that is not minuscule compared with what lies outside of it.

The crisis facing the tourist industry, with its travel agents, airlines, hotel chains, guides, tours, packages, cruises, reserves, excursions and promotions, does not threaten travel as such. However, what threatens tourism can also threaten the material, logistical and economic conditions that make travel possible. Just as we should distinguish the traveller from the tourist, we should not confuse an indifference to the crisis in tourism with a contempt for the difficulties of travel. Safeguarding the significance of travel is even more important when the climate crisis demands we travel less. The challenge is not to stop travelling, but to travel less and better.

*

Prevented or discouraged from travelling, we have felt the desire to return to the places we visited in the past. We have even missed the 'non-places' that must be traversed to reach them: airports, stations, motorways, planes, trains, cars. There is a thrill in the experience of taking a flight or a train or driving from one city to another that deserves attention. Exploring it invites us to reconsider the distinction introduced by French anthropologist Marc Augé between 'places' and 'non-places'. 'If a place can be defined as relational, historical, and concerned with identity', he argues, 'than a space which cannot be defined as relational, or historical, or concerned with identity will be a non-place', thus being 'surrendered to solitary individuality, to the fleeting, the temporary and ephemeral'.[7]

Augé's analysis of the non-place draws on the fact that spaces such as airports, shopping centres and hotel chains are filled with words and texts of prescriptive, prohibitive or informative character, which discourage interaction with other individuals and local communities.[8] Granting anonymity, the non-place prompts alienation and disaffection. Yet, during the global quarantine, who has not found themselves remembering past travels by air, train or car in which, at once distracted and concentrated, they reviewed past relationships and memories, took life-changing decisions or made plans for the future? Some might even remember brief but meaningful conversations with fellow travellers.

There is no doubt that airports and stations are spaces in which subjectivity circumvents benchmarks of culture and history, but this does not necessarily make them spaces of self-alienation, automated reflection or indifference to the other. In fact, we should guard against allowing the dissection of the non-place to become an apology for the principle of identity that underpins its opposite: the place, as a historically and culturally defined location. In *Empire*, after examining 'how exploitation and domination constitute a general non-place on the imperial terrain',[9] Antonio Negri and Michael Hardt devise 'a new task' to be placed at the heart of contemporary politics: 'the concrete invention of a first *new place in the non-place*',[10] that is, the task of 'constructing ontologically new determination of the human'.[11] Perhaps, then, we should try to imagine the 'non-identity' of the 'non-place', along with the appeal of nomadism, not as the absence of dwelling, but as the promise of happiness inherent in any departure, mingled with the hope of finding and building a home elsewhere.

*

During quarantine, some people travelled on the internet. The idea is not new, and since Google Street View appeared in 2007, several photographers have explored its artistic potential. The platform has allowed for a possibility that could be designated meta-photography: the photographing of the photographed world. Meta-photographers select, enlarge, cut, edit and collate vistas, not of the world as the photographer found it and decided to capture it, but of photographic reproductions produced in an automatic and haphazard way by the revolving cameras mounted on the roofs of cars or attached to the rucksacks of pedestrian travellers by Google.

Thomas, the protagonist of the film *Blow Up* (1966), by Antonioni, is also drawn to explore the random: a photograph he took that appears to inadvertently evidence a crime. He is a character in whom the roles of spectator, artist, detective, voyeur and spy converge. Unlike Thomas, however, the meta-photographer eschews the element of capture: they do not *take*, they only *retake* photographs. They are at once *the person who looks at* and *the person who takes* the photograph, but in a very particular way: they take the photograph they see more than they see the photograph they take.

What are the aspects that draw the meta-photographer to the photographed world? One of the photographer Michael Wolf's best-known projects is a serialization of 'unfortunate events', such as accidents, mistakes and fires.[12] Artist and film-maker Jon Rafman goes in search of the unexpected, the unusual and the shocking.[13] Photographer Doug Rickard explores the evidence of abandonment at the peripheries of cities.[14] Tending towards the subversive, the motivations of the photographers who use Google Street View often intersect with the polemics that platform provokes, from those concerning its possible predatory uses and opportunistic abuses to those relating to the privacy of the individuals photographed. Photographic uses of Google Street View can also concern travel *negatively*, as when they arise directly from the impossibility of travelling. The meta-photographic projects 'The Agoraphobic Traveller' by Jacqui Kenny and 'The Lonesome Traveller' by David Cachopo are both born of the impossibility of travel; in one case because of a phobia, in the other because of a pandemic.[15]

Undertaken during the first months of the coronavirus pandemic, 'The Lonesome Traveller' project is a succinct illustration of the fact that travel is *irremediable*. On the one hand, it presents a fictional journey from Lisbon to Vik, Iceland, treating it as a journey, but also as a fiction. The traces of the 'it is as if' are everywhere: in the Google watermark, the colour gradient at the upper and lower margins of the photographs, the blurred-out faces and registration marks, the asymmetries in the juxtapositions of images and the reflection of the camera itself on mirrored surfaces. On the other hand, not aiming to, or being able to, simulate a real journey, this fictional meta-photographic journey has the effect of intensifying and transforming our desire to travel, sharpening our awareness of its role as an opening to the unexpected encounter with the other.

The traveller made solitary by meta-photography eventually finds himself accompanied: the people he encounters in the photographs he takes or re-takes seem possessed of a strange vivacity. Their gestures, though paralysed, seem to reach out to the traveller, to express complicity. They too stand at thresholds, stare at maps, hurry over crossings, hesitate at junctions, have accidents, select shortcuts. Through a multiplicity of images, an imaginary community of travellers emerges. The journey of the meta-photographer is both more and less than what it seems to be: less because it is not a substitute for a journey that did not happen; more because it announces a journey that is still to come.

Study

In a text entitled 'Requiem for the Students', Agamben deplores what he considers to be 'the end of student life as a form of existence'.[16] Of the conjunction of practices that mark university life, which do not just include attending classes and participating in seminars, but also socializing and collective research, he says 'all this, which has lasted for almost ten centuries, is now ending – forever'.[17] His repugnance for what he calls 'technological barbarity', associated with the 'increasingly pervasive diffusion of digital technologies', leads him to assert that 'instructors who agree – as they have done *en masse* – to subject themselves to the new online dictatorship and to hold all their classes remotely are the exact equivalent of those university professors who, in 1931, pledge allegiance to the Fascist regime'.[18]

It is curious, then, to note how closely Agamben follows some of the ideas advanced by Heidegger, including that of technology being 'the extreme danger',[19] in this text. On 21 April 1933, shortly after Hitler had been sworn in as Chancellor of Germany, Heidegger was elected rector of the University of Freiburg. Not only did he not decline the nomination, he enrolled in the Nazi Party soon after, on 1 May 1933. Agamben's lament emulates an older model too. When he affirms that 'part of the technological barbarism that we are currently living through is the cancellation from life of any experience of the senses as well as the loss of the gaze, permanently imprisoned in a spectral screen',[20] he revives Plato's 'pharmacological anxieties', that a deterioration of memory and a numbing of thought would result from the transition from the oral to the written.

What makes Agamben's analogy unfortunate is not just the hyperbole of comparing the recourse to digital platforms to give classes in the context of a pandemic in 2020 with the connivance with fascist and Nazi regimes in the 1930s, but also the inappropriateness of the assumption on which this comparison is based – namely, that technology is inherently dangerous. This text by Agamben is an overt example of the way legitimate worries about the dispersal and destabilizing of the student community or the potential for exploitation of distanced learning by institutions can become entangled with conjectures of a nostalgic and conservative hue. Agamben uses the expression 'technological barbarism' as if it were an analytical judgement, as if the affinity between technology and barbarism were irresistible, as if every form of technology, if only because it fosters 'forgetfulness', must inevitably lead to barbarism. In doing so, he closes off any possible exploration of those aspects of the digital revolution that can impact on study by offering new opportunities for autonomy or intervention.

*

The dispute has deepened at universities in the wake of the pandemic. On one side is the propaganda of those who push for the digital modernization of teaching and learning; on the other, the invective of those who fear the debasement of higher education at the hands of the new barbarians of the digital age. While the former provoke outrage and exasperation by embracing the changes in a subservient and uncritical manner, as if they were updating software, the latter rarely fail to disappoint in their inability to imagine the scope and depth of the true problem. Too often, the debate becomes captive of the rhetoric of command: who is in charge of the university? The bureaucrats at the Education Ministry or the full professors of the academic world? That is, however, *not* the question – at least when it comes to study.

We live in an age of information deluge. Never before in the history of humankind – and this phenomenon is increasing exponentially – has an epoch accumulated and had access to so much data. As Roberto Simanowski puts it, 'data love' is not without dangers, and these are not restricted to issues of privacy and safety.[21] Knowledge itself, the ensemble that constitutes its conditions of possibility, is under threat. The problem is not Wikipedia itself, but the assumption that Wikipedia renders a theoretical class obsolete. The problem is the failure to distinguish between the challenge of learning and teaching and the task of gathering information. Another problem – perhaps the most crucial – is that of spiralling entropic tendencies, a rapid conjunction of dispersion and accumulation of knowledge that seems to engulf the very possibility of making sense of where we stand historically and politically.[22]

What threatens the possibility of study, then, is not the same thing that threatens the prestige of higher education institutions. In defending themselves from the alleged debasement brought about by digital media by enforcing more 'rigour', more 'seriousness', more 'specialization', universities run the risk of becoming fully absorbed into the productivity-obsessed model of capitalism. With that comes entropy, the true menace to knowledge, and a growing sense of disorientation that prevents knowledge from being constituted. This would be a Pyrrhic victory for the university: an avoidance of a 'fall into the mud' at the price of becoming irrelevant.

Before embracing or rebelling against the digital revolution in the universities, taking sides with either the 'moderniser' or the 'conservative', we need to staunch the blood flowing from a pre-existing wound. To do this, we need to identify the aggressor as capitalist productivism. If blind pursuit of productivity and subservience to the laws of the market have no remedy, then our universities are already doomed and the digital poison is irrelevant.

*

It might be helpful to take a detour and turn to the collective work of Fred Moten and Stefano Harney, published in *The Undercommons: Fugitive Planning & Black Study*. Two of the main aspects of this book are a critique of the university system and a reimagining of the concept of study. 'It cannot be denied', they argue, 'that the university is a place of refuge, and it cannot be accepted that the university is a place of enlightenment'.[23] It is true that the university fosters thought, incentivizes research and permits divergence. It is however also true that, under pressure from capitalism, and operating as part of its machinery of credit and debt, the purpose of the university, measured by what it has to offer – or, increasingly, to sell – to students, is not emancipation *through* thought, but the professionalization *of* thought, in particular critical thought.

The challenge, for Moten and Harney, is one of attending the university in a subversive way: being *at* the university without being *of* the university. The intellectual who critiques the university with the aim of repairing or reforming it has succumbed to the logic of what they aim to critique. What the university and the critic of the university have in common is that both are oblivious to what is operating in the underground. It is there that the subversive intellectual must disappear, delving 'into the undercommons of enlightenment, where the work gets done, where the work gets subverted, where the revolution is still black, still strong'.[24]

Against the negligence of the critical intellectual Moten and Harney set the study undertaken by those who have joined the undercommons of enlightenment. Yet this study is far from consisting of 'intellectual' activities alone. Rather than summoning the foolish or the distracted or the exhausted to the classroom to endow their activities with an intellectual flavour, the point is to recognize the study that these activities already entail, as well as to dismantle the dichotomy between 'intellectual' and 'non-intellectual' labour. The labour that takes place in the undercommons of the university is predicated on radical equality, not just between the students – once the hierarchy between student and teacher has collapsed – but also between areas of study. Finally, when this collapse has been recognized and these distinctions have been unlearned, the challenge is the invention of escape, the drawing up of fugitive plans and to understand that escape can and should happen here and now.

For Moten and Harney, study, as a form of life in common, is the subterranean heart of the university. It is like a centrifuge spinning out into the areas that surround the classroom: corridors, terraces and cafes. Study is made up of encounters, clashes and collisions between people, objects, experiences, ideas and words. It is allergic to distance and draws pleasure from proximity. The metaphors for study are supremely tactile, but their very status as metaphors implies that these encounters, clashes and collisions denote experiences that do not necessarily presuppose co-presence in space and time.

In a recent interview, in answering a question about the impact of the pandemic on their collaborative work, Harney and Moten responded that 'when we are apart we are not alone'. The various ways of being together, remaining in contact and finding ourselves in synchrony can transcend the dichotomy between presence and absence:

When we are together we hang out. We have a good time. When we are separated we write together. So on the one hand these times are not that different. They are also not that different because we both hang out and write and struggle in the general emergency. In that emergency, the sirens have not stopped for 500 years. In that emergency, you shelter, but together, and not in place, but on the move. ...

We have neither advocated for the joys of the classroom, as if they were accessible to all and all good, nor have we abdicated our responsibility to radicalize that space for work and play; but neither have we either simply accepted the imposed protocols of distance learning or rejected them from the position of moralistic hedonism that professors often occupy and from which they often do their professing when they have what is generally thought to be a good job at a good school. Being on the move and in shelter together we try to work with what we got and with whom we're held, against the grain of this new imposition of scarcity but in enjoyment of the levelling it has induced.[25]

The crucial point is to counter the 'imposition of scarcity' while also recognizing and taking advantage of the 'levelling it has induced'. One thing does not exclude the other. In highlighting the 'moralistic hedonism' of professors, Moten and Harney pinpoint the way in which a lament for lost presence can become entangled with anxiety in the face of eroded authority.

On 7 July 2020 it was announced that legal residence in the United States for foreign students would be restricted to those whose classes took place in person. This is just one example among many of threats currently facing students. The 'shock', as Naomi Klein predicted, can be exploited not just to slash budgets and monetize absence, but also to discourage movement, close borders and stigmatize foreigners. It turns out that capitalism depends far less on movement than we thought it did: nothing is so static it cannot be liquefied and turned into profit. As Harney and Moten remind us, before technology permitted what we have come to call 'distanced learning', capitalism was already creating 'social distancing'.[26]

Study is to university what travel is to tourism. We take refuge at university to study, just as we accept tourism to travel. The risk is not of atrophy of the senses or forgetfulness of being. What must be defended passionately from the advances of capitalism is the possibility of flight and our understanding of its necessity. Never before has a union between students and travellers beneath the banner of what Harney and Moten call 'fugitivity' felt more like a burning duty.

Community

The idea that the pandemic offers 'a good opportunity' to change the world does not convince Rancière. It is far from clear that the pandemic signals the triumph of biopower or heralds the emergence of a digital dictatorship, or that it has weakened the capitalist system. Rancière is sceptical about the hopes placed by many on the 'moment after' (*moment d'après*), the moment in which we would see an end to inequality or a change in our civilizational paradigm. Holding out for this 'moment after', he warns, amounts to a complacent and consoling illusion. The hallmark of this illusion is the tendency to announce that transformation is imminent while remaining silent on 'who will do everything that needs to be done to change everything'.[27]

The future, Rancière reminds us, is constructed from the dynamics of the present. When the pandemic is over, governments will return to their routine, and the challenge will remain of identifying 'the forces able to connect the fight against the forces of exploitation and domination to the invention of another future'.[28] This question, though decisive, is not new, and, as Rancière highlights, a period of confinement may not be the best time to resolve it. 'It's not obvious', he concludes, 'that the confinement has made us go far in that direction [of the invention of another future]'.[29] In this sense, Rancière agrees with Badiou, who, when the pandemic hit, saw nothing new beneath the contemporary sky.

Rancière is skilled at deconstructing some of the most categorically optimistic and pessimistic interpretations of the pandemic, but his analysis overlooks the extent to which the conditions of the formation of collective subjects have mutated. He reminds us that the pandemic, far from ushering in major transformations, has been used as a pretext by the most authoritarian states to order their police to clean up the streets. We are advised not to forget that 'stay at home' and 'get off the streets' mean the same thing. While this observation is pertinent, the assumption that the street constitutes a necessary and sufficient condition for contemporary political transformation seems to be misleading.

Rancière does not say so explicitly, but his often-expressed doubt that 'the best time to reflect on a worldwide phenomenon be that when we find ourselves isolated from the world',[30] beyond presupposing that the world stops at the front door, points to a hope – deceptive because its focus has become obsolete – that the street is the principal arena for that transformation.

*

Elias Canetti's monumental work, *Crowds and Power*, offers an interpretation of the phenomenon of the crowd that centres around the dialectic of proximity and distance. Canetti sees the impulse that leads to the formation of the crowd as the reversal of the fear of contact. The release provided by the crowd acts to liberate the individual from their fear of being touched, and of the threat of attack inherent in it. The crowd, according to Canetti, also liberates the individual, in a sense that is particularly relevant in modern societies, from the yoke of the distances that work both to protect and to imprison them:

> A man stands by himself on a secure and well defined spot, his every gesture asserting his right to keep others at a distance. He stands there like a windmill on an enormous plain, moving expressively; and there is nothing between him and the next mill. All life, so far as he knows it, is laid out in distances – the house in which he shuts himself and his property, the positions he holds, the rank he desires – all these serve to create distances, to confirm and extend them. ...
>
> But the satisfaction of being higher in rank than others does not compensate for the loss of freedom of movement. Man petrifies and darkens in the distances he has created. He drags at the burden of them, but cannot move. ...
>
> Only together can men free themselves from their burdens of distance; and this, precisely, is what happens in a crowd. During the discharge distinctions are thrown off and all feel *equal*. In that density, where there is scarcely any space between, and body presses against body, each man is as near the other as he is to himself; and an immense feeling of relief ensues. It is for the sake of this blessed moment, when no-one is greater or better than another, that people become a crowd.[31]

This passage exemplifies one of the fundamental characteristics of Canetti's conception of the crowd, namely the equality – comforting, although temporary, and consequently illusory – of the individuals that comprise it. Canetti, in contrast with Gustave Le Bon or Sigmund Freud, does not see the crowd as implying hierarchy or presupposing leadership. The military and the church, offered by Freud as paradigmatic examples of the crowd, occupy a secondary role in Canetti's analysis. His crowd forms suddenly, grows uninhibitedly and disperses as rapidly as it formed. Even the crowds that take a 'closed' form – those created through domestication by religions or reification by nation states – fear the crowd in its 'open' or 'wild' form. This conception of the crowd that forms spontaneously, without leader or direction, can assist us in analysing initial reactions to the pandemic.

Given its planetary scale and the speed of its appearance, the fear of the pandemic could be said to be the first truly global crowd experience. There was no corner of the planet in which the alarm did not sound. While the optimists spoke of global solidarity, for the pessimists this was no more than positive externality: it was not solidarity but the fear of not being safe that was producing a global surge of emotion. Either way, Canetti's study is still of significant interest today insofar as it conceptualizes the conditions of crowd formation as an informal and disordered process, occurring in a moment that precedes leadership, at once resisting and inviting the manipulation of the leader. In our current context, however, in which the gathering of the multitude is taking place virtually, the question arises as to whether we can still talk of a crowd. Is it still a crowd when there is no contact? What kind of 'discharge' will relieve the multitude today?

Byung-Chul Han offers a reimagining of the crowd for a post-digital world. In the age of what McLuhan has called *Homo electronicus*, the multitude was summoned and engaged by the mass media, such as radio and television, informational forms characterized by a dynamic of unidirectionality. In our present age of *Homo digitalis*, the new media, starting with the internet, are more suited to interactive and therefore multidirectional forms of communication and information flow. This has changed the nature of the crowd: it is no longer a herd or a pack. Like something from a Kafka story, it has awoken to find itself transformed into a swarm:

> The new mass is the *digital swarm*. Its features distinguish it radically from the *crowd* – the classical form that the many assumed. ...

The digital swarm lacks the soul or spirit of the masses. Individuals who come together as a swarm do not develop a *we*. No harmony prevails – which is what welds the crowd together into an active entity. …

Today's *Homo digitalis* is anything but 'nobody'. He retains his private identity, even when forming part of the swarm. Although he expresses himself anonymously, as a rule he has a *profile* – and he works ceaselessly at optimizing it. Instead of being 'nobody', he is insistently *some-body* exhibiting himself and vying for attention. The mass-mediated nobody, on the other hand, does not claim attention for himself. His private identity is extinguished. He has vanished into the mass.[32]

The swarm is a crowd stripped of both body and soul. It does not go in *one* direction, does not speak with *one* voice, does not develop a 'we'. It is a grouping of individuals, who each have their own profile and never stop being individuals, coming together at a specific moment, virtually, as a swarm. The 'someone' that is each individual cannot become completely 'no one': the individual is imprisoned inside their profile and their project. They cannot physically experience the discharge and relief of being swallowed up by the crowd. This is the source of their resentment. The decision to take refuge in anonymity and the tendency, under anonymity, to become vitriolic, are manifestations of this resentment. Although bleak, these reflections on the metamorphosis of the crowd into a swarm cannot be ignored at a moment when we are seeking to explore the possibility of constructing a 'we' for the post-digital world, a 'we' that might be able to become an agent of change.

*

All community is imagined. It can only be devised, experienced or felt by being imagined by people who do not know each other and between whom there is no personal, emotional or intellectual proximity. This is the argument advanced by historian Benedict Anderson, for whom it is an error to think that the imagination of national communities is grounded on real communities. The nation, he argues, 'is *imagined* because the members of even the smallest nation will never know most of their fellow-members, meet them, or even hear of them, yet in the minds of each lives the image of their communion'.[33] The significance of Anderson's theory, however, transcends the framework of nations and nationalities. *All community is imagined.* What applies to national identity also applies to class, gender and racial identity, as well as to whatever 'we' might constitute itself as a subject of change.

Anderson's argument that *any community is imagined* might be extended today to assert that *any imagined community is remediated.* All community, to the extent to which it is imagined – that is, the extent to which it forms around images that are the crystallization of shared ways of thinking and feeling – is also remediated. No image escapes remediation. No image dodges the digital condition. Hence, no imagined community can avoid the dangers of digitalization, including the paradox of the swarm: the isolation of the individual inside the virtual multitude. The pandemic has exacerbated this paradox, for as Peter Szendy points out, 'ademia, the empty streets of panendemic times … goes hand in hand with an unprecedented upsurge in the proliferation of images'.[34]

The challenge remains one of the imagination, but the street, in which the multitude transforms into a crowd, is no longer the principal arena. It is not, of course, that the multitude has stopped going out into the street – as the anti-racism demonstrations following the assassination of the Afro-American George Floyd by a white policeman in Minneapolis attest – but that even the street is now remediated. The crowd immediately summons its avatar to enable the demonstration to continue online: on Facebook and Twitter, those who were and those who were not present at the demonstration can react and comment on the event, thus prolonging it. Unless the swarm prolongs the event in this way, the demonstration birthed by the crowd is stillborn.

At the same time, if the crowd can summon the swarm, the swarm can also summon the crowd. This is how the anti-racist protests in the wake of Floyd's assassination were able to turn global with such speed and vehemence. Good ideas – anti-racist or ecological – can turn viral too. The process of this viralization is so slippery and malleable, however, that we can never take our eyes off it for long.

*

In his *Confessions,* Rousseau relates a strange episode in his life when, arriving in Genoa by sea when plague had just broken out in Messina, he had to choose between spending fourteen days in quarantine on board ship with the rest of the crew, or staying in complete isolation in a building (a *lazaretto*) without furniture. The philosopher opted for the isolation, describing with humour how he transformed his scant luggage and possessions into a makeshift bed, table and chair, attained an acceptable level of comfort and was able to stroll around the huge premises unrestricted.

In her discussion of the Covid-19 pandemic, Catherine Malabou revisits this passage from *Confessions*. Exploring the dilemma faced by Rousseau, she comments that she too would opt for isolation, but notes that it is a double isolation, a quarantine within a quarantine:

There is something else perhaps more profound in this passage, which is that quarantine is only tolerable if you quarantine from it – if you quarantine within the quarantine and from it at the same time, so to speak. The lazaretto represents this redoubled quarantine that expresses Rousseau's need to isolate from collective isolation, to create an island (*insula*) within isolation. Such is perhaps the most difficult challenge in a lockdown situation: to clear a space where to be on one's own while already separated from the community. Being cooped up on a boat with a few others of course generates a feeling of estrangement, but estrangement is not solitude, and solitude is, in reality, what makes confinement bearable. And this is true even if one is already on one's own. I noticed that what made my isolation extremely distressing was in fact my incapacity to withdraw into myself. To find this insular point where I could be *my self* (in two words). I am not talking here of authenticity, simply of this radical nakedness of the soul that allows to build a dwelling in one's house, to make the house habitable by locating the psychic space where it is possible to *do* something, that is, in my case, write. I noticed that writing only became possible when I reached such a confinement within confinement, a place in the place where nobody could enter and that at the same time was the condition for my exchanges with others. When I was able to get immersed in writing, conversations through Skype, for example, became something else. They were dialogues, not veiled monologues. Writing became possible when solitude started to protect me from isolation.[35]

Malabou's observations are not just a reformulation of what other thinkers, from Nancy to Žižek, have pointed out: that in the periods of global quarantine, the preoccupation with the other manifested itself through self-isolation. Malabou's point is at once simpler and more nuanced. Enforced company is more than merely inconvenient or ill-advised; it can also be painful, even unbearable, in that it prevents us from finding a habitable mental and physical space. Without that, it is impossible to find a sense of community. If it is true that 'solitude cannot be the origin of society', it is also true, Malabou concludes, that 'it is necessary to know how to find society within oneself in order to understand what politics means'.[36]

Art

We must expect great innovations to transform the entire technique of the arts, thereby affecting artistic invention itself and perhaps even bringing about an amazing change in our very notion of art.

— PAUL VALÉRY[37]

Art is an encounter with the enigmatic – that which resists interpretation, recognition or assimilation. Although the dance of capture and escape that characterizes the aesthetic experience goes beyond the domain of perception, it remains vulnerable to shocks affecting the empirical conditions under which artistic practices take place. One of these shocks has been that they can no longer rely on place.

Since the beginning of 2020, social distancing measures have drastically affected conditions of artistic production and reception. They have demanded the closure, followed by reopening with restrictions, of museums, galleries, cinemas, cultural centres and performance venues. It is not just access to these places by the public that has been curtailed: activities such as filming sessions, production meetings and rehearsals have also been cancelled or delayed. Although the crisis affects every art form, the situation is particularly delicate for the performing arts, not just because they require the gathering of actors and audience for public performance but also because they often require frequent rehearsals.

It did not take artists, companies and institutions long to turn to the internet. They began to make ad hoc recordings and archival material available online, and the use of live-streaming took root. Platforms such as Zoom became popular, permitting not only contact between artists and the public but also between artists themselves, to rehearse, jam or discuss – all at a distance. The lack of presence inevitably led to anxieties and questions. While some lamented the impossibility of physical contact because, in theatre and dance in particular, it had made a large proportion of projects unviable, others began to ask wryly whether it might in fact be possible to conduct a concert or a rehearsal – whether of a symphony by Gustav Mahler or a string quartet by Béla Bartók – without the interaction *in loco* of the musicians.

This question was not merely a technical one about clarity of image or sound or immediacy of transmission on a platform such as Zoom. It was also about what is understood by music, theatre or dance and the nature of the relationship of these art forms with technologies of audiovisual reproduction and remediation. Reiterating a common position amongst those working in the performing arts, the director Olivier Py said in an interview that 'theatre is communion' and 'real presence, not just of the actors but also of the audience', to such an extent that 'the union at the time of a concert or a performance is of the order of the sacred'.[38] Aside from its theological overtones, Py's assertion recalls the analyses made by Peggy Phelan in the 1990s. Phelan says that 'performance cannot be saved, recorded, documented, or otherwise participate in the circulation of representations *of* representations'.[39] Thought of in this way, the situation for the performing arts in the pandemic context appears not just worrying but catastrophic.

*

Thus begins another episode in the saga of the clash between the 'apocalyptic' and the 'remediated'. The apocalyptic aesthete fears the end of art, or at least of art forms such as music, theatre and dance, understanding that the essence of these art forms is only fulfilled in a live performance in front of an audience. A concert or rehearsal on Zoom is, at best, a contradiction in terms, at worst an aberration. The remediated aesthete naturally disagrees. While for the apocalyptic aesthete nothing can be good if it cannot satisfy the prerequisite of co-presence between artists and public, for the remediated aesthete nothing can be bad if it involves some kind of technological mediation. According to the remediated aesthete, we are seeing not the end of the arts, but merely the turning of a page in their history, which only a prophet of doom would interpret as some kind of catastrophe.

The mistake made by the apocalyptic aesthete is the adoption of a purely naturalistic conception of art; the assumption, explicit or implicit, of a state of naturalness that technology will taint. Excluding technology from the history of the arts, however, is both inaccurate and leads to insoluble contradictions. To take the case of music, if we excluded technological processes for the capturing, fixing, editing, generating and reproduction of sound, we would have to banish experiences of *musique concrète*, which uses recorded sounds; and electronic music, which uses synthesized sounds, from the category of music. While we might praise them as ingenious, we would be declaring the works of Pierre Schaeffer and Karlheinz Stockhausen, to name two representatives of the above-mentioned trends, or the pianola pieces by Conlon Nancarrow, not to be music. This would be even more applicable to the newer practices of turntablism and sampling.

While apocalyptic aesthetes can be accused of naturalism, remediated aesthetes can be accused of naivety. They turn a blind eye to the real problems afflicting the arts: the threats to the material or institutional survival of its actors from the interruption of the circuit of production and reception to the loss of the key dynamic of in-person collaboration. The fact that we cannot exclude technology from our conception of art does not mean that its intervention is immediately and necessarily pertinent from an artistic point of view, nor that we can designate it the solution to all problems. In the context of the restrictions imposed by the pandemic, merely appealing to the 'capacity for reinvention' of artists, as a pretext for showing ourselves favourable to technology, is equivalent to reproducing the neoliberal rhetoric of 'creativity and innovation' while ignoring the fact it has been misappropriated from the discourse of the arts.

It is neither a question of taking sides between the apocalyptic and the remediated nor of seeking a compromise between the two. More important than describing their explicit opposition is uncovering their implicit convergence. Both conceive of remediation as a remedy for distance. The apocalyptic complains because the remedy does not cure the disease: however seamless the remediation, it lacks the authenticity of the original experience. The remediated counters that the remedy does alleviate the symptoms: better a reproduction of the original experience than no experience at all. While their conclusions diverge, the assumption they rest on is the same: that the purpose of remediation is to reproduce all that the original experience can offer as faithfully as possible: the allure of presence in the here and now, the unpredictability of live experience, the authenticity of communion between performers and audience.

*

A passage from *The Logic of Sense* by Gilles Deleuze might shed more light on this unexpected convergence between the proponents and the detractors of the curative properties of remediation. In a discussion of Nietzsche's critique of Plato, Deleuze argues that, contrary to what is often supposed, the crux of the Platonic argument is not so much a distinction between the world of ideas and the world of phenomena as a distinction, at the level of the phenomenon, between good and bad copies. When an action is proclaimed just, Socrates asks, what definition of justice allows it to be recognized, validated or authorized as such? The Platonic argument combines the hypothesis of an 'original' with an insistence on the establishment of the status and claim of its 'copies'.[40]

Deleuze's analysis suggests that the validation offered to the copy by virtue of its similitude to the original is acquired at the price of servility. The good copy, faithful to the original, is not free to deviate from what it is and should purport to be: an image. As an image, it cannot be, and should not purport to be, neither more nor less than that which it is an image of. It should limit itself to reproducing the original without adding anything or leaving anything out. Such is the virtue of the image in which Deleuze suspects the good copy's servility. To return to our apocalyptic and remediated aesthetes, both are still too Platonic. In elevating the similarity of copy (remediation) and original (co-presence) to an ideal, while disagreeing only in terms of their appraisal of how successful the copy is in emulating the original, they reduce the debate to a farcical cataloguing of the pros and cons of Zoom.

In other words, both the credulity of the remediated aesthete and the scepticism of the apocalyptic aesthete stem from an overly superficial conception of how fruitful the relationship between art and technology can be. The real alternative is not between acceptance and rejection of the new media, but between more or less creative, more or less audacious, more or less divergent uses of technology – including digital technologies – in artistic practice. Not the least of the dangers of the pandemic lies in the assumption that, concomitant to the polemic between defenders and opposers of the recourse to the digital, the proliferation of live-streams and the sharing of content evidence a deepening of the artistic potential of technology in relation to the arts. The 'Zoomification' or 'Youtubeification' of artistic practices and objects should not be mistaken by a more creative use of technology.

The debate only becomes interesting when we recognize that the dichotomy between the apocalyptic and remediated views does not do full justice to the potential of the relationship between art and technology. If we can talk of a disruption of the sense of art, we must admit that the effects thereof, which are not restricted to a clash between 'authenticity' and 'democratization', extend beyond the sphere of reception. What might resemble abstract speculation has concrete implications for artistic practice and creation, especially when it comes to the vast, singularly complex universe of interpretation: from live or recorded performance, to stage or film direction to the audiovisual remediation of musical, theatrical or dance productions.

*

The situation currently being experienced in the field of opera – a proverbially problematic art form, almost always improbable, outrageous in its own way – is a useful yardstick for the exploration of some of these ideas. On the one hand, opera is one of the art forms most affected by the pandemic, being, despite its reputation for elitism, highly collaborative. It requires close and frequent meeting and interaction, not only between different art forms but also between different people with different competencies and personalities, including librettists, composers, producers, directors, conductors, singers, musicians and technicians. But opera is also one of the art forms that reacted most swiftly and dynamically to the crisis. The explanation for this apparent contradiction lies in the recent history of the genre. Being commonly seen as unpopular and on the decline to the point of becoming obsolete, opera has, over the last few decades, engaged in intense dialogue with new media.

The case of New York's Metropolitan Opera is paradigmatic. The transmission of opera performances to cinemas all over the world has been one of the company's hallmarks since Peter Gelb became its artistic director in 2007. When the pandemic demanded the cancellation of both live performances and cinecasts, everything shifted to the company's website. The series 'The Met: Live in HD' gave way to 'Nightly Opera Streams' of more and less recent productions by the company. A gala event – an 'At-Home Gala' to be more precise – was also organized and live-streamed on 25 April 2020. With Peter Gelb and Yannick Nézet-Séguin (who replaced James Levine as musical director of the company in 2018) as hosts, this gala, at once homely and global, included live-stream performances of dozens of singers all over the world, as well as the pre-recorded Zoom videos of orchestral and choral pieces performed at a distance by members of the orchestra and choir of the company, directed by Nézet-Séguin. These included the Prelude to Act III of Wagner's *Lohengrin* and the 'Chorus of Hebrew Slaves' (the famous '*Va, pensiero*') from Verdi's *Nabucco*.

It is fair to say that Gelb was simply doing what he had to do considering the profile of the opera company he leads. If I dwell on the case of the Met, it is not to praise or to criticize it, but to illustrate the ambivalence of such initiatives: their virtue is also a danger. The 'Nightly Opera Streams' and the 'At-Home Gala' aim to find a compromise between the commitment to technology and the praise of liveness. The Met puts its faith, in an unequivocal and straightforward way, in technologies of remediation, while at the same time affirming that the 'real thing' happens live. Given the circumstances, this position is not reprehensible. In a broader discussion, we might explore whether the emphasis on the marvels of technological innovation does conceal conservatism in terms of programming, commissioning and dramaturgy. In any case, we should not forget that the artistic potential inherent in the interaction between opera and technology goes far beyond initiatives of this type. It would be absurd to reduce the myriad possibilities for innovation associated with the relationship between the two to the transmission of past performances or live private recitals in which the loss of presence and immediacy is compensated for by a glimpse of the artist's room.

At the end of a virtual round table discussion at the 2020 edition of the Aix-en-Provence Festival, Pierre Audi chose the phrase *tabula rasa* as best characterizing the spirit of the current times for the arts in general and opera in particular. As a description of that year's online version of the festival, it might seem hyperbolic. However, it sets the tone for the approach that could and should emerge from this crisis, based on an understanding that the use of technologies of remediation is an intrinsic part of the challenge of imagining new ways of experiencing, interpreting and creating. Rather than culminating in strategies for expanding the public, responses to the pandemic crisis have exposed the inseparability of technological innovation *and* interpretative and creative inventiveness.

Recent, but pre-pandemic, productions, such as Puccini's *Tosca* by Christophe Honoré, at the Aix-en-Provence Festival, and Wagner's *Tannhäuser* by Tobias Kratzer, at the Bayreuth Festival, both from 2019, illustrate how the use of technology at its most challenging is about more than just expanding audiences. The transmission of *Tosca* on the culture channel Arte in 2019 and its free availability on the festival's website in 2020 were certainly important, as was the live cinecast of the premiere of *Tannhäuser* at various locations in Germany and other European countries (the production is now available on DVD and Blu-ray). However, the debate is diminished and incomplete if we do not also consider the incursion of technologies of remediation into the live spectacles themselves, as well as the remarkable extension of the palette of interpretive strategies that stem from what Philip Auslander calls the interpenetration between mediatization and liveness.[41]

Through the use of technologies that allow for the projection of filmed material, either archival, pre-recorded or captured direct at the moment of performance, the productions of *Tosca* and *Tannhäuser* become reflections on the operatic genre itself. In Honoré's *Tosca*, this centres around the figure of the diva, and serves to highlight the violence that surrounds and pursues her, which is also that of the operatic institution and tradition themselves. We experience the character in duplicate: as well as seeing and hearing the soprano Angel Blue giving the vocal performance of Floria Tosca, we also accompany soprano Catherine Malfitano, both on stage, where she embodies the 'old diva' (a character that does not exist in the original work), and on screen, in the video projection of Andrea Andermann's famed television production of 1992, in which the same Malfitano starred as Tosca. This creates a fascinating dissolution of boundaries between past and present, stage and screen, reality and fiction. Kratzer's *Tannhäuser* explores similar ground by drawing a parallel between the circle of singers of Wartburg and the structure of the Bayreuth Festival itself, the esotericism of which the production exposes and subverts. This is achieved through the inclusion of new characters – the dwarf and the drag queen – and by drawing attention to the spaces both inside and outside the theatre, made literal through the juxtaposition of live filming and pre-recorded material: the images and voices of the characters in the gardens of the Festspielhaus are made immediately visible and audible to the audience by being shown on a screen above the stage.

*

The pandemic is not only a *threat* to but also an *opportunity* for the performing arts. What I mean by opportunity in this context should be clear from the start. I am not suggesting that the difficulties are in themselves an opportunity. However, analysis of the artistic answers that have been proposed to circumvent the constraints associated with social distancing reveals that these answers are prompting new, potentially fruitful questions about what it means to experience, to perform and to create music, theatre, dance and opera. In other words, the restrictions, inasmuch as they have forced artists, performers and institutions to find previously undreamed-of solutions to unprecedented problems, are also stimulating artistic imaginations. Again, the field of opera appears exemplary. As a new season began in many countries in September 2020, some venues reopened, allowing a number of live performances to be seen. But the peculiarities of the new offerings could not but cause a stir.

Barrie Kosky's production of Mussorgsky's *Boris Godunov*, which premiered on 20 September 2020 at the Zurich Opera House, is a case in point.[42] Mussorgsky's masterpiece is no chamber opera. It is a grand opera requiring an immense orchestra and chorus. How could such a performance be possible in the age of Covid-19, especially considering how small the orchestra pit is and how close to each other the members of the chorus are when performing on stage? The production team came up with a unique answer to this question. Instead of adapting the original score, they changed its means of presentation. While the singers performed on stage in front of the audience, the orchestra and chorus performed in the rehearsal room, one kilometre away from the theatre, which allowed for the necessary distance among musicians and singers. The sound was live-streamed into the theatre, which required a state-of-the-art fibre-optic communication system, including multiple cables connecting the two venues and no less than nineteen loudspeakers, controlled by a sound engineer in the theatre. Meanwhile, the image of the conductor, directing the orchestra and the chorus in the rehearsal room was projected in the theatre, enabling the singers to follow the gestures of the conductor and perform accordingly. Finally, at the beginning and the end of the performance, the image of the rehearsal room was projected onto a big screen in the theatre, so the audience could applaud the musicians as well.

This production triggered different reactions from the critics who attended the performance in the theatre. 'I had my doubts', John Rhodes comments, 'as to sight and sound beforehand but have to say that I was highly impressed'.[43] Reflecting on the invisibility of the orchestra, he goes as far as to compare this production with those at the Bayreuth *Festspielhaus*. Laura Servidei is less enthusiastic and evokes the feeling of a karaoke night. 'What we witnessed in Zurich', she admits, 'was a small technological miracle. ... The experience, however, was not comparable to a live performance. ... [T]he sound didn't feel natural. ... I couldn't help thinking that an opera in concert version, with the musicians distancing on the stage, would have served the art better than this solution'.[44] In any case, this was an entirely new way of performing opera, one in which liveness and mediatization, presence and absence, distance and proximity, were blended in the context of a live performance.

Yuval Sharon, the new artistic director of Detroit's Michigan Opera Theater, faced a similar challenge: that of presenting a large-scale opera, this time by Richard Wagner, while adhering to social-distancing measures. His solution was even more radical, in that it involved leaving the opera house entirely (which may sound strange in general, but is not so strange in the case of Sharon, considering his previous productions with the Industry in Los Angeles).[45] *Twilight: Gods*, as the work was called, took place, not in the opera house but in the parking garage across the street.[46] The production can be characterized as a drive-through adaptation of Wagner's *Twilight of the Gods*. The audiences drove through the building, parking in each of its storeys for the duration of one scene, while listening to the music on their radios and watching the performers from their cars. When they reached the upper terrace, the show culminated with Brünnhilde's emulation scene set against the backdrop of the Detroit's skyline.

What is at play in this production is more than logistical pragmatism or marketing strategy to make opera popular again. Sharon's *Twilight: Gods* is about sixty minutes long, about a quarter of the duration of Wagner's *Twilight of the Gods*. The adaptation involved various and radical alterations of the original, from reducing the score, not only in terms of length but also in terms of instrumentation, to devising an abridged version of the plot. The result is a re-creation of Wagner's opera rather than the re-presentation that a traditional stage production would be, no matter how innovative or radical its staging. While issues of fidelity are widely discussed in opera criticism – the controversies around *Regieoper* being one example – they are often polarized around the question of how the plot is reinterpreted and represented on stage. Even in the more provocative stagings, such as those of Peter Konwitschny or Calixto Bieito, the score is left untouched.[47] From this point of view, it would not be far-fetched to suggest that the pandemic provided an opportunity to develop a more radical concept of what it means to reinterpret, to represent and, finally, to recreate a pre-existing opera.

My third example is a production of *L'enfant et les sortilèges*, the one-act opera that Ravel composed to a libretto by Colette in the 1920s. Produced by Virtual Opera Project, a recently created contemporary opera company led by Rachael Hewer, this new version was also informed by pandemic-related constraints. However, while in the cases of Kosky and Sharon we are talking about a live performance, in the case of Hewer we are talking about a film. Andrew Clements, writing in *The Guardian*, praised it as 'one of the most successful online operas I've come across over the last nine months'.[48] This new version of Ravel's *fantaisie-lyrique*, in a re-orchestration of the score for twenty-seven players, brought together the London Philharmonic Orchestra, led by conductor Lee Reynolds, and more than eighty performers, all of whom, throughout the course of year, had participated in rehearsals and recordings remotely. Hewer constructed a home-made green-screen studio out of her garden shed, using the FX technique to overlay the recorded cast's singing faces with captured movement in an unique and imaginative operatic version of body-doubling.

As Hewer says in an interview, 'this production is not only a response to the opera itself, but to the situation we find ourselves in now'.[49] The bored, rebellious child of the original opera (played on screen by Amelie Turnage and sung by the mezzo Emily Edmonds) is being home-schooled during lockdown: her tantrum includes smashing the laptop she is supposed to be working at, and at one point her fantasy takes her into an accident and emergency department. Opera on screen is not new (whether in the form of the recording of a stage production, the film production of a pre-existing opera or the original film opera). What is new about this production is the fact that the actual making of the film involved the collaboration of a myriad performers from all over the world, who under normal circumstances would either work together in the same place or would not work together at all.

In one way or another, all of these productions reimagine the operatic form: by blurring the boundary between liveness and remediation, by radicalizing the interpretative and creative context of performance and by challenging the myth of medium-specificity. Their merit, which transcends the solutions they advance, consists in the questions they raise about the musical-theatrical genre, questions that unsettle our perception not only of the social role of opera but also of its very mediality and its relation to other arts.

*

The UK theatre director Simon McBurney was due to direct *Wozzeck* by Alban Berg at the Aix-en-Provence Festival in 2020. When the decision was made in May 2020 to cancel the production, the festival organizers made a recording of *The Encounter*, one of McBurney's previous works, available online. *The Encounter* was a multimedia piece produced by McBurney's theatre company Complicité and premiered in London in 2015. As McBurney explains in his introductory statement, filmed during quarantine and ingeniously juxtaposed with the video of the recording, the piece explores the theme, disturbingly relevant to the 2020 experience, of the links between individual isolation and collective destiny. Also relevant is the centrality of audiovisual technologies to the show, which invites its audience to embark on an individual experience for which they must use headphones, while seated in an auditorium surrounded by hundreds of other people.

The Encounter theatricalizes a true story that has already been told in literary form: a journey to the heart of the Amazon jungle by the US photo-journalist Loren McIntyre, a long-term collaborator with *National Geographic*. McIntyre photographed the source of the Amazon river in the Peruvian Andes in 1971, and, in 1969, made contact and lived for several weeks with a Mayoruna tribe. In 1987, he recounted this remarkable experience to the Romanian writer Petru Popescu, who used it as the basis for his book *Amazon Beaming*, first published in 1991. This is the narrative that *The Encounter* takes as its inspiration. In 2014, McBurney visited the Amazon himself and spoke to a Mayoruna group about the piece he was working on. He also met Popescu, who gave him his personal impressions of McIntyre, who died in 2003.

To tell this adventure story in *The Encounter*, McBurney makes use not just of his talents as an actor but also a significant battery of technology. The most unusual of these is binaural technology, which allows the recording and reproduction of sound in 3D, meaning sound can be located all around the listener, and distance and proximity can be suggested. This function is just one element in a complex web of technological wizardry in which sounds and voices produced live coexist with pre-recorded sounds, sound effects created by the manipulation of different microphones and the use of electronics in real time. Though a few visual effects are used, for instance to create a scene of a fire at the indigenous camp, *The Encounter* is principally a sound-based piece, in which the story is told through the layering of voices, sounds and noises. It is a piece in which illusion is at once constructed *sonorously* and deconstructed *visually* (as we hear the rustle of dry leaves under the feet of McIntyre, we see McBurney shaking a box filled with the magnetic tape from VHS cassettes).

However, *The Encounter* is more than just a story told through a series of varyingly complex and ingenious auditory special effects. It is also an interplay between reality and fiction, used by McBurney to ask existential and civilizational questions about time, space and community. This interplay affects and involves itself in the 'reality' of the 'fiction' itself. The piece juxtaposes moments when McBurney 'represents' McIntyre – running through the forest, taking photographs, breathless, trembling, delirious – and moments in which he 'represents' himself, months before, when his daughter, whose recorded voice we also hear, interrupts his work sessions at night to ask her father to tell her another story before she falls asleep. The frontier between reality and fiction is never clear, not even from the perspective of McIntyre, or what remains of his perspective following mediation from Popescu, McBurney and myself recounting this. The communication between McIntyre and the tribal chief, for example, takes place without words through telepathy. Is this a hallucination? The experience of immersion in nature, for which the photographer set out prepared – not just with camera, clothes and supplies, but with ideas and convictions, too – is also an experience of divestment, disorientation and delirium.

McIntyre's journey happens in time as well as in space. The space-time web begins to entangle him when the tribe explains that the journey of their community will take them in the direction of the 'beginning'. They tell him they must escape in search of the past, having become trapped in the present by threats to their existence in the form of approaching civilization. This is how McBurney describes the space-time experience McIntyre has with the Mayoruna:

> The main feature of time, by western definition, is its passage. But for the Mayoruna, McIntyre tells Popescu, time is at once mobile and static. It moved with man, stopped with him, advanced and retreated with him. It is not the implacable judge, condemning man to a tragically brief life. Time is a shelter, an escape into safety and regeneration, a repository whose chief function is not piling up the past, intact yet dead, but rather keeping it alive and available. And, in the face of violent encroachment on their land by white settlers, that past assisted them with an alternative to a menacing present.

But, as McIntyre discovered, it was not only his notions of time that were challenged, but also those of distance – crucially the distance between one person and another – for these ideas were communicated to him in a startling way. Wordlessly. In one extraordinary act of communication, the concept of a 'separate self', so precious to our contemporary sense of identity, is undermined to the point that it becomes, for McIntyre, utterly illusory. One self, one so-called individual consciousness, he discovered, can be more connected to another in ways he had never imagined, ways we are blind to in 'our' world. A world which paradoxically supposedly connects us, through technology, more than at any time in history.

'We are going to the beginning', he is told, or rather believes he is told, because this phrase is communicated without words.

'What beginning?'

'The beginning. Are you coming with us?'

With no way of returning to his camp or contacting others, McIntyre has no option but to follow his 'captors' on this journey to 'the beginning'. It leads to a ritual that will take him and his hosts across a barrier into another time. That of 'the beginning', when there are no white people, no settlers; to the beginning of the Mayoruna people, to ensure their survival. His return from this experience forms the end of the story I am telling.[50]

Just as McIntyre finds himself captured by the Mayoruna and compelled to follow them on their journey to the beginning, we, as captive spectators, follow McBurney in his revisitation of it. Both journeys are imagined, but the one McBurney invites us to make – or obliges us to make, whether in an auditorium or at home, as soon as we put the headphones on – leads us to imagine contact, touch and immersion in nature through the medium of dense technology. As well as being thought-provoking and moving, *The Encounter* offers a fascinating paradox: while it tells of an experience of loss of self, spiritual contact and immersion in nature, as well as of the absolute stripping away of artefacts, it does this by means of a performance saturated with technological media that employs every possible type of device and instrument of audiovisual reproduction and remediation.

The performance invites us to allow ourselves to be captured by the questions it raises: How do we relate to the remote in time and space? What touches us? How do we affect and how are we affected? What do we fear? What do we desire? What are we looking for? Why are we running away? Where do we want to get to? Where, how and with whom do we feel at home? McBurney could not have asked these questions the way he did, because he could not have evoked the experiences that make them feel unavoidable, without making provocative, ingenious and intelligent use of a vast array of technologies.

This meeting of a meditation on our destiny on the earth and the contradictions of our civilization with the use of the most advanced audiovisual technology makes this performance emblematic of the way dialogue can take place between technology and ecology. We follow in our own footsteps, as we search for and allow ourselves to be captured by the distant only to encounter it within ourselves, thus diverging from ourselves and rediscovering ourselves as part of the world. The use of technology in *The Encounter* raises questions that have nothing to do with the danger of losing who we are and everything to do with the hope – even the expectant joy – of encountering what we can be.

Beyond the pandemic

Let's return to a question posed at the beginning of this book: *what will become of us after the pandemic?* Having reached this point, engaging with that question might – and probably should – exasperate us. What does that 'after' mean, and when will it begin? Has it not already begun? Is it not indistinguishable, irrespective of the declared end of the pandemic, from a now that feels more urgent than ever? Most importantly, who is meant by 'us'? Is it the 'us' of humanity as a whole, as this crisis is global? Can we really conceive of a universal 'us' in a world made up of societies crippled by inequality? Does that 'us' actually mean the inhabitants of so-called developed countries, where the use of digital technologies has in fact increased? Is it even more specifically Western countries? How can we interrogate the suspicion that, in formulating these questions in these ways, we have already fallen short?

Conscious of the difficulties and uncertainties to which these questions attest, this book has chosen to dispense with the *a priori* determination of an 'us': by evoking it from the beginning, it aims not to presuppose it but to invite its elaboration. This leads me to another problem with the question *what will become of us after the pandemic?* It imagines us as passive. We should instead be asking *what will we do with ourselves after the pandemic?* The need to transcend the dichotomy of optimism and pessimism exists not just at the level of diagnosis but also as we explore the tension between 'interpretation' and 'transformation' to blur the frontier between passivity and activity. The friction between optimism and pessimism can generate a short circuit that prompts us not just to face what is happening, but to intervene.

Although describing radical changes, this book rejects a narrative of miraculous transformations. The pandemic has not changed human nature, whether we conceive of it with the image of the 'bon sauvage' or the 'Homo homini lupus'. It has not changed the fundamental nature of institutions, even if it has compelled them to make unprecedented decisions. It is questionable that it has contributed to the fall of capitalism, at least not in the terms in which this has been suggested. If there is 'optimism' in this book, it is of a more modest variety, which consists of raising the question *what will we do with ourselves?*, while emphasizing that the composition of that 'we' is something we cannot assume but must work to elaborate. Which 'us' and 'we' do we want to develop after the pandemic? My response at the end of this book, which I recognize as precarious but feel to be urgently required, is that the 'us' and 'we' that are needed are of a sort that will bring us as close as possible to the distant, an 'us' and a 'we' imagined as a counter to isolation and localism.

*

In *The Human Condition*, Hannah Arendt characterizes the alienation of the modern world as a 'twofold flight from the earth into the universe and from the world into the self'.[1] Despite moving in opposite directions, both flights express the consciousness of the modern subject. The individual who, out of concern for their own safety and well-being, becomes indifferent to the destiny of humanity (world alienation) is the same as the one who dreams of escaping the planet (earth alienation).

The dialectic between the world and the earth might help us to understand the sense in which the pandemic is inextricably bound to the digital revolution. It might also illuminate the challenges that lie ahead. What Arendt sensed, writing that 'speed has conquered space' and 'has made distance meaningless',[2] and what Sloterdijk sums up when he affirms that 'the human race has reached a situation of synchronicity on the basis of a stream of information' and that we are 'living more and more in the same time dimension'[3] is in fact the hallmark of the pandemic shock: the sense that has spread across the planet that we live in a technologically globalized world.

Viewed in this way, the pandemic has laid bare the paradox of globalization. From the perspective of the conditions of human experience, the pandemic, and the acceleration of the digital revolution that came with it, have pushed globalization to the point at which it fulfils itself entirely. At the level of collective consciousness and sensibility, however, the pandemic reveals globalization as a contradictory and, in its political and ecological dimensions, failed project. The challenge that now faces humanity is no less than a realignment of the 'world' with the 'earth', the discovery of a new capacity to imagine the planet as our home.

Such global consciousness and sensibility do not exist in the abstract. We must create the connections, establish the links and construct the pathways that make them concrete. It is a political error to think they can be built from purely local experiences. The major danger of anti-globalist thinking is that, on the pretext of a necessary critique of world capitalism, it transforms itself into provincial universalism, a collection of reasonable ideas discussed in a common language with fellow countrymen in a Facebook bubble.

The danger stems not just from the trapping of experience and thought inside a local or national sphere, but also from the ceding of the imaginary terrain, where our feelings of belonging, caring, hope, enthusiasm and happiness thrive, to the local or national imagination. Independently of the ideas being defended – and even when defending the most rigorous universalism – anti-globalism runs the risk of contributing to the nationalist and capitalist egotism it aims to fight.

Ecological thinking itself depends on a global consciousness and sensibility. This recalls the Gaia hypothesis, which demands a shift of perspective from the unbounded universe to the bounded, superficial, atmospheric planet. It entails a narrowing of focus from the abstraction of the infinite universe to the concrete of the finite planet, with its fragile coverings that shelter us. This narrowing of focus, from universe to planet, on the plane of what we *know*, will only bear fruit on the plane of what we *want* if it is accompanied by a widening of focus, from our own country to the planet, on the plane of what we *love*.

The leap from 'I' to 'we' – or better, from a local or national 'I' and 'we' to a global 'I' and 'we' – will not come about through conviction alone, but through experiences: of study, art, travel, love and community. Only these can turn the awareness and sensibility of a global 'we' into something concrete. In our current times, this global awareness and sensibility *also* depend on technology. The connections, links and pathways at planetary level will not emerge in isolation from the digital milieu. Hence the importance of the alliance between technology, ecology and politics that a critical vision of the digital should help us to imagine and elaborate.

The global tumult that greeted the beginning of the pandemic has given way to moral attrition and inertia. While major restrictions were still in place, resentment, exasperation and despair have gained ground. In the long-running soap operas of case numbers and infection or vaccination rates (exercises in navel-gazing by each individual country), the rhetoric has pivoted towards national sentiment. The alarming increase in xenophobia and intolerance, while inarguably arising from social and historical contexts specific to particular countries, has also been fed by the trapping of the imagination inside the perimeters of the nation state. It is authoritarianism, racism and nationalism, not technological dystopia, that should be our greatest fears. While these threats are not mutually exclusive, it is becoming more and more apparent that today's exorcism of technology is creating a smoke screen behind which the greatest danger – which is not the obliviousness of being but its paranoid and deadly contraction – can grow.

Technology is not a remedy: it is not a substitute for the presence of the other, for movement over the earth, for multi-sensory experience, for the gathering of the many, for the experience of the here and now. But in a historical moment in which the close is closing in, it allows us to keep sight of the beacon and the spark that the experience of the distant can provide. We owe it to the future not to allow those energies to be extinguished.

NOTES

Prologue

1   Jay David Bolter and Richard Grusin, *Remediation: Understanding New Media* (Cambridge, MA and London: MIT Press, 1999), 45.

2   Ibid., 2–15.

3   Jacques Derrida, *Of Grammatology*, trans. and with a preface by Gayatri Chakravorty Spivak (Baltimore and London: Johns Hopkins University Press, 1997), 141–316. Crucial in Derrida's argument is the insight that speech is supplemented not only by writing, which is 'the supplement *par excellence*' (281), but also by gesture. It is this recognition – given that gesture, which accompanies and precedes speech, can also be seen as a form of writing – that undermines the assumption that speech is more 'original' and 'natural' than writing.

4   Marshall McLuhan, *Understanding Media: The Extensions of Man*, with an introduction by Lewis H. Lapham (Cambridge, MA and London: MIT Press, 1994).

5   Immanuel Kant, *Critique of Pure Reason*, trans. and ed. Paul Guyer and Allen W. Wood (Cambridge: Cambridge University Press, 1998), 273.

6   See, for instance, Slavoj Žižek, *Pandemic!: COVID-19 Shakes the World* (London and New York: OR Books, 2020); Slavoj Žižek, *Pandemic! 2: Chronicles of a Time Lost* (London and New York: OR Books, 2020); Giorgio Agamben, *Where Are We Now? The Epidemic as Politics*, trans. Valeria Dani (London: Eris, 2021) [originally published as *A che punto siamo? L'epidemia come politica* (Macerata: Quodlibet, 2020)]; Bruno Latour, *Où suis-je? Leçons du confinement à l'usage des terrestres* (Paris: La Découverte, 2021); Donatella Di Cesare, *Immunodemocracy: Capitalist Asphyxia*, trans. David Broder (Cambridge, MA and London: MIT Semiotext(e)/ Intervention Series 30, 2021) [originally published as *Virus sovrano? L'asfissia capitalistica* (Turin: Bollati Boringhieri, 2020)].

7 The original version was published in Portugal by Documenta (in December 2020) and in Brazil by Elefante (in August 2021).

Chapter 1

1 Giorgio Agamben, 'The Invention of an Epidemic' [originally published in *Il Manifesto* on 26 February 2020], in *Where Are We Now? The Epidemic as Politics*, trans. Valeria Dani (London: Eris, 2021), 12–14.

2 Giorgio Agamben, 'Reflections on the Plague' [originally published in the Quodlibet blog on 27 March 2020], in *Where Are We Now? The Epidemic as Politics*, trans. Valeria Dani (London: Eris, 2021), 21.

3 Ibid.

4 Vladimir Safatle, 'Para além da necropolítica', *Pandemia Crítica*, N-1 edições, 2020. Available online: https://www.n-1edicoes.org/textos/191 (accessed 31 March 2021). In this article, Safatle draws on Mbembe's concept of 'necropolitics' to characterize the Brazilian government's disastrous management of the pandemic. See also Achille Mbembe, *Necropolitics*, trans. Steven Corcoran (Durham, NC and London: Duke University Press, 2019).

5 Karl Marx, 'Theses on Feuerbach', trans. Loyd D. Easton and Kurt H. Guddat, in *Selected Writings*, ed. Lawrence H. Simon (Indianapolis, IN and Cambridge, MA: Hackett, 1994), 101.

6 Theodor W. Adorno, *Negative Dialectics*, trans. E. B. Ashton (London and New York: Routledge, 2004), 3.

7 Franco 'Bifo' Berardi, *The Second Coming* (Cambridge, UK: Polity Press, 2019), 3.

8 Slavoj Žižek, *Pandemic!: COVID-19 Shakes the World* (London and New York: OR Books, 2020), 39–41.

9 Ibid., 40.

10 Ibid., 41.

11 In using the term 'suspicion', I have in mind the way in which Ricœur employs it, when he gives Marx, Nietzsche and Freud the title of 'masters of suspicion'. However, contrary to Ricœur, I do not use the term pejoratively. Rather, I want to suggest that hypotheses *and* suspicions are equally intrinsic to philosophical reasoning. See Paul Ricœur, 'The Conflict of Interpretations', *Freud and Philosophy: An Essay on Interpretation*, trans. Denis Savage (New Haven, CT and London: Yale University Press, 1970), 20–36.

12 Byung-Chul Han, 'The Viral Emergency and the World of
Tomorrow', trans. Richard James Bowling. *Pianola Con
Libre Albedrío*, 29 March 2020. Available online: https://
pianolaconalbedrio.wordpress.com/2020/03/29/the-viral-emergence-
y-and-the-world-of-tomorrow-byun-chul-han/ (accessed 10 February
2021).

13 See Naomi Klein, *The Shock Doctrine: The Rise of Disaster
Capitalism* (Toronto: A. A. Knopf, 2007).

14 See Isabelle Stengers, *In Catastrophic Times: Resisting the Coming of
Barbarism*, trans. Andrew Goffey (Lüneburg: Meson Press, 2015).

15 Žižek, *Pandemic!*, 39.

16 Byung-Chul Han, 'The Tiredness Virus', *The Nation*, 12 April
2021. Available online: https://www.thenation.com/article/society/
pandemic-burnout-society (accessed 15 May 2021). See also Byung-
Chul Han, *The Burnout Society*, trans. Erik Butler (Stanford, CA:
Stanford University Press, 2015).

Chapter 2

1 Alain Badiou, 'On the Epidemic Situation', trans. Alberto Toscano,
Verso [blog], 23 March 2020. Available online: https://www.
versobooks.com/blogs/4608-on-the-epidemic-situation (accessed 31
March 2021).

2 Peter Szendy, 'Viral Times', *Critical Inquiry* 47, no. 2 (Winter 2021)
[originally posted on the Critical Inquiry blog, 15 April 2020].
Available online: https://critinq.wordpress.com/2020/04/15/viral-
times/ (accessed 31 March 2021).

3 Pedro Duarte, *A Pandemia e o Exílio do Mundo* (Rio de Janeiro:
Bazar do Tempo, 2020), 13.

4 See Roberto Esposito 'Cured to the Bitter End' [originally published
in *Antinomie* on 28 February 2020], in *Coronavirus, Psychoanalysis,
and Philosophy: Conversations on Pandemics, Politics, and Society*,
edited by Fernando Castrillón and Thomas Marchevsky (New York:
Routledge, 2021), 28–9; and Latour, *Où suis-je?*

5 See Mark Fisher, *Capitalist Realism: Is There No Alternative?*
(Winchester: Zero Books, 2009); and Klein, *The Shock Doctrine*.

6 Fisher, *Capitalist Realism*, 16.

7 Bruno Latour, 'What Protective Measures Can You Think of so We
Don't Go Back to the Pre-crisis Production Model?', trans. Stephen

Muecke. Bruno Latour, 2020. Available online: http://www.bruno-latour.fr/node/853.html (accessed 31 March 2021).

8 Judith Butler, 'Capitalism Has its Limits', Verso [blog], 30 March 2020. Available online: https://www.versobooks.com/blogs/4603-capitalism-has-its-limits (accessed 31 March 2021).

9 Bruno Latour, 'Bruno Latour: "This is a global catastrophe that has come from within"' (interview conducted by Jonathan Watts), *The Guardian*, 6 June 2020. Available online: https://www.theguardian.com/world/2020/jun/06/bruno-latour-coronavirus-gaia-hypothesis-climate-crisis (accessed 31 March 2021).

10 Jordi Carmona Hurtado, 'Componer con Gaia: el problema de la libertad en tiempos del coronavirus', *El salto diario*, 23 March 2020. Available online: https://www.elsaltodiario.com/el-rumor-de-las-multitudes/componer-con-gaia-el-problema-de-la-libertad-en-tiempos-del-coronavirus (accessed 31 March 2021).

11 Markus Gabriel, 'We Need a Metaphysical Pandemic', Uni Bonn, 26 March 2020. Available online: https://www.uni-bonn.de/news/we-need-a-metaphysical-pandemic (accessed 31 March 2021).

12 Hurtado, 'Componer con Gaia'.

13 Naomi Klein, 'Screen New Deal', *The Intercept*, 8 May 2020. Available online: https://theintercept.com/2020/05/08/andrew-cuomo-eric-schmidt-coronavirus-tech-shock-doctrine/ (accessed 31 March 2021).

14 David Harvey, 'Anti-Capitalist Politics in the Time of COVID-19', *Jacobin*, March 2020. Available online: https://jacobinmag.com/2020/03/david-harvey-coronavirus-political-economy-disruptions (accessed 31 March 2021).

15 Donatella Di Cesare, *Immunodemocracy: Capitalist Asphyxia*, trans. David Broder (Cambridge, MA and London: MIT Semiotext(e)/Intervention Series 30, 2021), 6.

16 Ibid., 16.

17 Achille Mbembe, 'The Universal Right to Breathe', trans. Carolyn Shread, *Critical Inquiry* 47, no. 2 (Winter 2021) [originally posted on the Critical Inquiry blog on 13 April 2020]. Available online: https://critinq.wordpress.com/2020/04/13/the-universal-right-to-breathe/ (accessed 15 July 2021).

18 Ibid.

19 Peter Sloterdijk, 'Co-Immunism in the Age of Pandemics and Climate Change' (interview conducted by Nathan Gardels), *Noema*, 12 June 2020. Available online: https://www.noemamag.com/co-immunism-an-ethos-for-our-age-of-climate-change/ (accessed 8 July 2021).

20 Jacques Rancière, 'Uma boa oportunidade?', trans. Peter Pál Perbart, N-1 edições. Available online: https://www.n-1edicoes.org/textos/72 (accessed 31 March 2021).

21 Badiou, 'On the Epidemic Situation'.

22 José Tolentino Mendonça, 'Redescobrir o poder da esperança', *Expresso*, 22 March 2020.

23 Jean-Luc Nancy, 'Communovirus' [originally published in *Libération* on 25 March 2020], trans. David Fernbach, Verso [blog], 27 March 2020. Available online: https://www.versobooks.com/blogs/4626-communovirus (accessed 31 March 2021).

24 Tomás Maia, 'O comum dos mortais (pensar a quarentena mundial)', *Revista Dobra*, Desdobramento pandemia, 2020, 7.

25 Roberto Esposito, *Immunitas: protezione e negazione dela vita* (Turin: Einaudi, 2002).

26 Peter Sloterdijk, *You Must Change Your Life: On Anthropotechnics*, trans. Wieland Hoban (Cambridge, UK: Polity Press, 2013).

27 Sloterdijk, 'Co-Immunism in the Age of Pandemics and Climate Change'.

28 Paul B. Preciado, 'Learning from the Virus', trans. Molly Stevens. Art Forum, May/June 2020. Available online: https://www.artforum.com/print/202005/paul-b-preciado-82823 (accessed 25 March 2021).

29 José Gil, 'A pandemia e o capitalismo numérico' [originally published in *Público* on 12 April 2020], *O Tempo Indomado* (Lisbon: Relógio d'Água, 2020), 105–6.

30 Preciado, 'Learning from the Virus'.

31 Cf. Institute for Health Metrics and Evaluation (IHME), 'COVID-19 Projections'. Available online: https://covid19.healthdata.org/global (accessed 14 November 2021); and World Health Organization (WHO), 'WHO Coronavirus (COVID-19): Overview'. Available online: https://covid19.who.int/ (accessed 14 November 2021).

Chapter 3

1 Han, 'The Viral Emergency and the World of Tomorrow'.

2 Karl Marx, *Grundrisse*, trans. Ben Fowkes (Harmondsworth: Penguin, 1993), 107.

3 Herbert Blau, *Blooded Thought: Occasions of Theater* (New York: Performing Arts Journal Publications, 1982), 121.

4 Marx, *Grundrisse*, 107.

5   Walter Benjamin, 'The Work of Art in the Age of Its Technological Reproducibility', second version, trans. Edmund Jephcott and Harry Zohn, in *The Work of Art in the Age of Technological Reproducibility, and Other Writings on Media*, edited by Michael W. Jennings, Brigid Doherty and Thomas Y. Levin (Cambridge, MA and London: Belknap Press of Harvard University Press, 2008), 23.

6   For commentary on these two particular examples, see Walter Benjamin, 'Little History of Photography', trans. Edmund Jephcott and Kingsley Shorter, in *The Work of Art in the Age of Technological Reproducibility, and Other Writings on Media*, edited by Michael W. Jennings, Brigid Doherty and Thomas Y. Levin (Cambridge, MA and London: Belknap Press of Harvard University Press, 2008), 276; and Michel Chion, *Sound: An Acoulogical Treatise*, trans. and with an introduction by James A. Steintrager (Durham, NC and London: Duke University Press, 2016), 131.

7   Marcel Proust, *The Guermantes Way & Cities of the Plain*, vol. 2, *Remembrance of Things Past*, trans. C. K. Scott Moncrieff and Terence Kilmartin (New York: Random House, 1981), 137.

8   John Berger, *Ways of Seeing* (London: Penguin, 1990).

9   Szendy, 'Viral Times'.

10   Maurizio Ferraris, *Mobilitazione Totale* (Rome: Laterza, 2015). See, for a summary in English, 'Total Mobilization', *The Monist* 97, no. 2 (April 2014), 200–221.

11   Harmut Rosa, *Unverfügbarkeit* (Salzburg: Residenz, 2018).

12   Szendy, 'Viral Times'.

13   Benjamin Noys, *Malign Velocities: Accelerationism and Capitalism* (Winchester, UK and Washington, DC: Zero Books, 2014), 103.

14   Alex Williams and Nick Srnicek, '#Accelerate: Manifesto for an Accelerationist Politics', in *#Accelerate: The Accelerationist Reader*, edited by Robin Mackay and Armen Avanessian (Falmouth: Urbanomic, 2017), 351.

15   Ibid., 356.

16   Noys, *Malign Velocities*, 103.

17   Jonathan Crary, *24/7: Late Capitalism and the Ends of Sleep* (London and New York: Verso, 2014), 127.

18   Emanuele Coccia, 'Reversing the New Global Monasticism', *Fall Semester*, 21 April 2020. Available online: https://fallsemester. org/2020-1/2020/4/17/emanuele-coccia-escaping-the-global-monasticism (accessed 1 June 2021). See also Emanuele Coccia, *Filosofia della casa: Lo spazio domestic e la felicità* (Turin: Einaudi, 2021).

19 Laurie Anderson, 'Spending the War Without You, Lecture 1: The River', The Norton Lectures, 10 February 2021. Available online: https://www.youtube.com/watch?v=6LuKgGn5e2g (accessed 20 December 2021).

20 Walter Benjamin, *Das Passagen-Werk, Gesammelte Schriften*, vol. 5.1, ed. Rolf Tiedemann (Frankfurt am Main: Suhrkamp, 1991), 560.

Chapter 4

1 Umberto Eco, *Apocalypse Postponed*, trans. Jenny Condie (Bloomington and Indianapolis: Indiana University Press, 1994).

2 Ibid., 19.

3 See Jacques Rancière, *The Emancipated Spectator*, trans. Gregory Elliott (London: Verso, 2009) and *The Ignorant Schoolmaster: Five Lessons in Intellectual Emancipation*, trans. Kristin Ross (Stanford, CA: Stanford University Press, 1991).

4 Rancière's view of the postmodern debate is rendered clear in the following passages of *Aesthetics and Its Discontents*: 'There is no postmodern rupture'. Postmodernism 'was simply the name under whose guise certain artists and thinkers realised what modernism had been: a desperate attempt to establish a "distinctive feature of art" by linking it to a simple teleology of historical evolution and rupture'. Jacques Rancière, *Aesthetics and Its Discontents*, trans. Steven Corcoran (Cambridge, UK: Polity Press, 2009), 42 and 49.

5 Eco, *Apocalypse Postponed*, 25.

6 See, for example, Bernard Stiegler, *The Age of Disruption: Technology and Madness in Computational Capitalism*, trans. Daniel Ross (Cambridge, UK: Polity Press, 2019); Paul Virilio, *Negative Horizon: An Essay in Dromoscopy*, trans. Michael Degener (London: Continuum, 2005); Shoshana Zuboff, *Surveillance Capitalism: The Fight for a Human Future at the New Frontier of Power* (New York: Public Affairs, 2019); Ferraris, *Mobilitazione Totale*; Byung-Chul Han, *In the Swarm: Digital Prospects*, trans. Erik Butler (Cambridge, MA and London: MIT Press, 2017); and Roberto Simanowski, *Data Love: The Seduction and Betrayal of Digital Technologies* (New York: Columbia University Press, 2016).

7 See György Lukács, *History and Class Consciousness: Studies in Marxist Dialectics*, trans. Rodney Livingstone (Cambridge, MA: MIT Press, 1971); and Zygmunt Bauman, *Liquid Modernity* (Cambridge, UK: Polity Press, 2000).

8 Bruno Latour, *Facing Gaia: Eight Lectures on the New Climatic Regime*, trans. Catherine Porter (Cambridge, UK: Polity Press, 2017), 184–219. It should be emphasized, however, that here I employ the notions of 'apocalyptical intellectual' and 'apocalyptical discourse' in Eco's sense (drawing on the opposition between 'integration' and 'apocalypse') rather than in Latour's when he mobilizes it in his ecologically oriented reflections.

9 Zuboff, *Surveillance Capitalism*, 15.

10 Yeshimabeit Milner and Amy Traub, 'Data Capitalism and Algorithmic Racism', Data for Black Lives/Demos, 2021. Available online: https://www.demos.org/research/data-capitalism-and-algorithmic-racism#What-is-Data-Capitalism? (accessed 1 July 2021).

11 Stiegler, *The Age of Disruption*.

12 Han, *In the Swarm*, 55–6.

13 Giorgio Agamben, 'Requiem for the Students' [originally published in the Quodlibet blog on 24 May 2020], *Where Are We Now? The Epidemic as Politics*, trans. Valeria Dani (London: Eris, 2021), 55.

14 Giorgio Agamben, 'The State of Exception has Become the Rule (Interview conducted by Nicolas Truong for *Le monde*)' [originally published in *Le Monde* on 28 March 2020], *Where Are We Now? The Epidemic as Politics*, trans. Valeria Dani (London: Eris, 2021), 26.

15 Di Cesare, *Immunodemocracy*, 90–1.

16 Friedrich A. Kittler, *Gramophone, Film, Typewriter*, trans., with an introduction, by Geoffrey Winthrop-Young and Michael Wutz (Stanford, CA: Stanford University Press, 1999), 1.

17 For a genealogy of the much-maligned format that revolutionized listening practices in the twenty-first century, see Jonathan Sterne, *MP3: The Meaning of a Format* (Durham, NC and London: Duke University Press, 2012).

18 Bolter and Grusin, *Remediation*, 3–15.

19 Bernard Stiegler, *Technics and Time*, vol. 2, *Disorientation*, trans. Stephen Barker (Stanford, CA: Stanford University Press, 2009), 2.

20 Ibid.

Chapter 5

1 Friedrich Nietzsche, *On the Genealogy of Morality*, ed. Keith Ansell-Pearson, trans. Carol Diethe (Cambridge: Cambridge University Press, 2006), 3.

2 Michel Foucault, *The Order of Things*, trans. Alan Sheridan (New York: Vintage Books, 1994), xiv.

3 Paul B. Preciado, *Countersexual Manifesto*, trans. Kevin Gerry Dunn (New York: Columbia University Press, 2018), 63.

4 Tim, 'Tinder and the Absent Date: The Modern Dating Philosophy', *Philosophy & Philosophers*, 15 February 2015. Available online: https://www.the-philosophy.com/tinder-absent-date-modern-dating-philosophy (accessed 15 July 2021).

5 Alain Badiou and Nicolas Truong, *In Praise of Love*, trans. Peter Bush (London: Profile Books, 2012), 6–7.

6 Han, *In the Swarm*, 22.

7 Marc Augé, *Non-Places: Introduction to an Anthropology of Supermodernity*, trans. John Howe (London and New York: Verso, 2008), 77–8.

8 Ibid., 94–101.

9 Michael Hardt and Antonio Negri, *Empire* (Cambridge, MA and London: Harvard University Press, 2000), 211.

10 Ibid., 216.

11 Ibid., 217.

12 See Michael Wolf, https://photomichaelwolf.com/#asoue/1 (accessed 16 November 2021).

13 See Jon Rafman, 'Selected Work', http://jonrafman.com/ (accessed 16 November 2021) and 9eyes, https://9-eyes.com/ (accessed 16 November 2021).

14 See Doug Rickard, 'A New American Picture', https://dougrickard.com/a-new-american-picture/ (accessed 16 November 2021).

15 See The Agoraphobic Traveller, https://www.theagoraphobictraveller.com/ (accessed 16 November 2021) and lonesometravelerproject, https://davidcachopo.com/lonesome-traveler-project (accessed 16 November 2021).

16 Agamben, 'Requiem for the Students', 55.

17 Ibid., 56.

18 Ibid.

19 Martin Heidegger, 'The Question Concerning Technology', in *The Question Concerning Technology and Other Essays*, trans. and with an introduction by William Lovitt (New York and London: Garland Publishing, 1977), 3–35, esp. 28–35.

20 Agamben, 'Requiem for the Students', 55.

21   Simanowski, *Data Love*.

22   For a systematic approach to the issue of entropy, illuminating the
need to counter entropy with negentropic strategies to tackle the
technological and ecological challenges that face humanity today,
see Bernard Stiegler, *The Neganthropocene*, ed., trans. and with
an introduction by Daniel Ross (London: Open Humanities Press,
2018).

23   Stefano Harney and Fred Moten, *The Undercommons: Fugitive
Planning & Black Study* (Wivenhoe, New York and Port Watson:
Minor Compositions, 2013), 26.

24   Ibid.

25   Fred Moten and Stefano Harney, 'When We Are Apart We Are Not
Alone' (interview conducted by Zach Ngin, Sara Van Horn and Alex
Westfall), *The College Hill Independent* 40, no. 10 (1 May 2020).

26   Ibid.

27   Rancière, 'Uma boa oportunidade?'.

28   Ibid.

29   Ibid.

30   Ibid.

31   Elias Canetti, *Crowds and Power*, trans. Carol Stewart (New York:
The Viking Press, 1962), 18–19.

32   Han, *In the Swarm*, 10–11.

33   Benedict Anderson, *Imagined Communities: Reflections on the
Origin and Spread of Nationalism*, revised edition (1983; London
and New York: Verso, 2006), 6.

34   Peter Szendy, 'Pandemia, Ademia, Iconodemia', Polemology [blog],
31 May 2021. Available online: https://polemologistblog.home.
blog/2021/05/31/peter-szendy-pandemia-ademia-iconodemia/
(accessed 20 July 2021).

35   Catherine Malabou, 'To Quarantine from Quarantine: Rousseau,
Robinson Crusoe, and "I"', *Critical Inquiry* 47, no. 2 (Winter 2021);
originally posted on the Critical Inquiry [blog], 23 March 2020; https://
critinq.wordpress.com/2020/03/23/to-quarantine-from-quarantine-
rousseau-robinson-crusoe-and-i/ (accessed 31 March 2021).

36   Ibid.

37   Paul Valéry, 'La conquête de l'ubiquité' (1928), in *Œuvres*, vol. 2,
Pièces sur l'art (Paris: Gallimard, 1960), 1283.

38   Olivier Py, 'La liturgie du théâtre n'a aucune différence avec celle
de la messe' (conversation with Anne-Laure Filhol), *La vie*; 29 June

2020. Available online: https://www.lavie.fr/ma-vie/culture/olivier-py-la-liturgie-du-theatre-na-aucune-difference-avec-celle-de-la-messe-1922.php (accessed 1 June 2021).

39	Peggy Phelan, *Unmarked: The Politics of Performance* (London: Routledge, 1993), 146.

40	Gilles Deleuze, 'Platon et le simulacre', in *Logique du sens* (Paris: Minuit, 1969), 292–306.

41	Philip Auslander, *Liveness: Performance in a Mediatized Culture* (1999; London: Routledge, 2008).

42	About this production, see Openhaus Zurich, 'Borus Godunow', https://www.opernhaus.ch/en/spielplan/calendar/boris-godunow/2020-2021/ (accessed 16 November 2021).

43	John Rhodes, 'Ingenious Performance of *Boris Godunov* at Zurich Opera, Current Envy of the Operatic World', *Seen and Heard International*, 22 September 2020. Available online: https://seenandheard-international.com/2020/09/ingenious-performance-of-boris-godunov-at-zurich-opera-current-envy-of-the-operatic-world/ (accessed 15 July 2021).

44	Laura Servidei, 'Technology to the Rescue in Zurich's New Stagings of *Boris Godunov*', *Backtrack,* 22 September 2020. Available online: https://bachtrack.com/es_ES/review-boris-godunov-kosky-karabits-volle-zurich-september-2020 (accessed 15 July 2021).

45	Site-specific productions are not new in Yuval Sharon's career. With the Industry, he directed *Hopscotch* and *Invisible Cities* in the streets and at the Union Station of Los Angeles.

46	About this production, see Michigan Opera, 'Twilight: Gods', 17 October 2020, https://michiganopera.org/season-schedule/twilight-gods/ (accessed 16 November 2021).

47	See, for example, David J. Levin, *Unsettling Opera: Staging Mozart, Verdi, Wagner, and Zemlinsky* (Chicago: University of Chicago Press, 2007).

48	Andrew Clements, 'Vopera's Brilliant Updating of Ravel Finds Wit and Relevance', *The Guardian*, 17 November 2020. Available online: https://www.theguardian.com/music/2020/nov/17/lenfant-et-les-sortileges-review-vopera-updating-ravel-video (accessed 15 July 2021).

49	Rachael Hewer, 'It's Always About Authentic Storytelling' (interview conducted by Catherine Kustanczy), *The Opera Queen*, 15 November 2020. Available online: https://www.theoperaqueen.com/2020/11/15/vopera-ravel/?curator=MusicREDEF (accessed 1 April 2021).

50 Simon McBurney, 'The Encounter: Simon McBurney on an Amazonian Voyage that Exploded Time', *The Guardian*, 11 February 2016. Available online: https://www.theguardian.com/stage/2016/feb/11/the-encounter-simon-mcburney-barbican-amazon-beaming-petru-popescu-loren-mcintyre (accessed 12 May 2020).

Epilogue

1 Hannah Arendt, *The Human Condition* (Chicago and London: University of Chicago Press, 1958), 6.

2 Ibid., 250.

3 Peter Sloterdijk, 'Humans Are Not Prepared to Protect Nature', *DW*, 23 June 2020. Available online: https://www.dw.com/en/how-do-we-change-peter-sloterdijk-environment-coronavirus-on-the-green-fence-climate-change/a-53533840 (accessed 15 July 2021).

BIBLIOGRAPHY

Adorno, Theodor W. *Negative Dialectics*. 1966. Trans. E. B. Ashton. London and New York: Routledge, 2004.

Agamben, Giorgio. *Where Are We Now? The Epidemic as Politics*. Trans. Valeria Dani. London: Eris, 2021. Originally published as *A che punto siamo? L'epidemia come politica*. Macerata: Quodlibet, 2020.

Anderson, Benedict. *Imagined Communities: Reflections on the Origin and Spread of Nationalism*. 1983. Rev. edn. London and New York: Verso, 2006.

Anderson, Laurie. 'Spending the War Without You, Lecture 1: The River'. The Norton Lectures, 10 February 2021. Available online: https://www.youtube.com/watch?v=6LuKgGn5e2g (assessed 20 December 2021).

Arendt, Hannah. *The Human Condition*. Chicago and London: University of Chicago Press, 1958.

Augé, Marc. *Non-Places: Introduction to an Anthropology of Supermodernity*. Trans. John Howe. London and New York: Verso, 2008.

Auslander, Philip. *Liveness: Performance in a Mediatized Culture*. 1999. 2nd edn. London: Routledge, 2008.

Badiou, Alain. 'On the Epidemic Situation'. Trans. Alberto Toscano. Verso [blog], 23 March 2020. Available online: https://www.versobooks.com/blogs/4608-on-the-epidemic-situation (accessed 31 March 2021).

Badiou, Alain and Nicolas Truong. *In Praise of Love*. Trans. Peter Bush. London: Profile Books, 2012.

Bauman, Zygmunt. *Liquid Modernity*. Cambridge, UK: Polity Press, 2000.

Benjamin, Walter. *Das Passagen-Werk, Gesammelte Schriften*. Vol. 5.1. Ed. Rolf Tiedemann. Frankfurt am Main: Suhrkamp, 1991.

Benjamin, Walter. *The Work of Art in the Age of Technological Reproducibility, and Other Writings on Media*. Ed. Michael W. Jennings, Brigid Doherty and Thomas Y. Levin. Cambridge, MA and London: Belknap Press of Harvard University Press, 2008.

Berardi, Franco. *The Second Coming*. Cambridge, UK: Polity Press, 2019.

Berger, John. *Ways of Seeing*. London: Penguin, 1990.

Blau, Herbert. *Blooded Thought: Occasions of Theater*. New York: Performing Arts Journal Publications, 1982.

Bolter, Jay David and Richard Grusin. *Remediation: Understanding New Media*. Cambridge, MA and London: MIT Press, 1999.

Butler, Judith. 'Capitalism Has its Limits'. Verso [blog], 30 March 2020. Available online: https://www.versobooks.com/blogs/4603-capitalism-has-its-limits (accessed 31 March 2021).

Canetti, Elias. *Crowds and Power*. Trans. Carol Stewart. New York: The Viking Press, 1962.

Castrillón, Fernando and Thomas Marchevsky (eds). *Coronavirus, Psychoanalysis, and Philosophy: Conversations on Pandemics, Politics, and Society*. New York: Routledge, 2021.

Chion, Michel. *Sound: An Acoulogical Treatise*. Trans. and with an introduction by James A. Steintrager. Durham, NC and London: Duke University Press, 2016.

Clements, Andrew. 'Vopera's Brilliant Updating of Ravel Finds Wit and Relevance'. *The Guardian*, 17 November 2020. Available online: https://www.theguardian.com/music/2020/nov/17/lenfant-et-les-sortileges-review-vopera-updating-ravel-video (accessed 15 July 2021).

Coccia, Emanuele. 'Reversing the New Global Monasticism'. *Fall Semester*, 21 April 2020. Available online: https://fallsemester.org/2020-1/2020/4/17/emanuele-coccia-escaping-the-global-monasticism (accessed 1 June 2021).

Coccia, Emanuele. *Filosofia della casa: Lo spazio domestic e la felicità*. Turin: Einaudi, 2021.

Crary, Jonathan. *24/7: Late Capitalism and the Ends of Sleep*. London and New York: Verso, 2014.

Deleuze, Gilles. *Logique du sens*. Paris: Minuit, 1969.

Derrida, Jacques. *Of Grammatology*. Trans. and with a preface by Gayatri Chakravorty Spivak. Baltimore and London: Johns Hopkins University Press, 1997.

Di Cesare, Donatella. *Immunodemocracy: Capitalist Asphyxia*. Trans. David Broder. Cambridge, MA and London: MIT Semiotext(e)/ Intervention Series 30, 2021. Originally published as *Virus sovrano? L'asfissia capitalistica*. Turin: Bollati Boringhieri, 2020.

Duarte, Pedro. *A Pandemia e o Exílio do Mundo*. Rio de Janeiro: Bazar do Tempo, 2020.

Eco, Umberto. *Apocalypse Postponed*. Trans. Jenny Condie. Bloomington and Indianapolis: Indiana University Press, 1994.

Esposito, Roberto. *Immunitas: protezione e negazione dela vita*. Turin: Einaudi, 2002.

Esposito, Roberto. 'Cured to the Bitter End'. In *Coronavirus, Psychoanalysis, and Philosophy: Conversations on Pandemics, Politics, and Society*, edited by Fernando Castrillón and Thomas Marchevsky, 28–9. New York: Routledge, 2021. [Originally published in *Antinomie* on 28 February 2020.]

Ferraris, Maurizio. *Mobilitazione Totale*. Rome: Laterza, 2015.

Ferraris, Maurizio. 'Total Mobilization'. *The Monist* 97, no. 2, Documentality (April 2014): 200–221.

Fisher, Mark. *Capitalist Realism: Is There No Alternative?* Winchester: Zero Books, 2009.

Foucault, Michel. *The Order of Things*. Trans. Alan Sheridan. New York: Vintage Books, 1994.

Gabriel, Markus. 'We Need a Metaphysical Pandemic'. Uni Bonn, 26 March 2020. Available online: https://www.uni-bonn.de/news/we-need-a-metaphysical-pandemic (accessed 31 March 2021).

Gil, José. *O Tempo Indomado*. Lisbon: Relógio d'Água, 2020.

Han, Byung-Chul. *The Burnout Society*. Trans. Erik Butler. Stanford, CA: Stanford University Press, 2015.

Han, Byung-Chul. *In the Swarm: Digital Prospects*. Trans. Erik Butler. Cambridge, MA and London: MIT Press, 2017.

Han, Byung-Chul. 'The Viral Emergency and the World of Tomorrow'. Trans. Richard James Bowling. *Pianola Con Libre Albedrío*, 29 March 2020. Available online: https://pianolaconalbedrio.wordpress.com/2020/03/29/the-viral-emergence-y-and-the-world-of-tomorrow-byun-chul-han/ (accessed 10 February 2021).

Han, Byung-Chul. 'The Tiredness Virus'. *The Nation*, 12 April 2021. Available online: https://www.thenation.com/article/society/pandemic-burnout-society (accessed 15 May 2021).

Hardt, Michael and Antonio Negri. *Empire*. Cambridge, MA and London: Harvard University Press, 2000.

Harney, Stefano and Fred Moten. *The Undercommons: Fugitive Planning and Black Study*. Wivenhoe, New York and Port Watson: Minor Compositions, 2013.

Harvey, David. 'Anti-Capitalist Politics in the Time of COVID-19'. *Jacobin*, March 2020. Available online: https://jacobinmag.com/2020/03/david-harvey-coronavirus-political-economy-disruptions (accessed 31 March 2021).

Heidegger, Martin. *The Question Concerning Technology and Other Essays*. Trans. and with an introduction by William Lovitt. New York and London: Garland Publishing, 1977.

Hewer, Rachael. 'It's Always About Authentic Storytelling' (interview conducted by Catherine Kustanczy). *The Opera Queen*, 15 November 2020. Available online: https://www.theoperaqueen.com/2020/11/15/vopera-ravel/?curator=MusicREDEF (accessed 1 April 2021).

Hurtado, Jordi Carmona. 'Componer con Gaia: el problema de la liberdad en tiempos del coronavirus'. *El salto diario*, 23 March 2020.

Available online: https://www.elsaltodiario.com/el-rumor-de-las-multitudes/componer-con-gaia-el-problema-de-la-libertad-en-tiempos-del-coronavirus (accessed 31 March 2021).

Institute for Health Metrics and Evaluation (IHME). 'COVID-19 Projections'. Available online: https://covid19.healthdata.org/global (accessed 14 November 2021).

Kant, Immanuel. *Critique of Pure Reason*. Trans. and ed. by Paul Guyer and Allen W. Wood. Cambridge: Cambridge University Press, 1998.

Kittler, Friedrich A. *Gramophone, Film, Typewriter*. Trans. and with an introduction by Geoffrey Winthrop-Young and Michael Wutz. Stanford, CA: Stanford University Press, 1999.

Klein, Naomi. *The Shock Doctrine: The Rise of Disaster Capitalism*. Toronto: A. A. Knopf, 2007.

Klein, Naomi. 'Screen New Deal'. *The Intercept*, 8 May 2020. Available online: https://theintercept.com/2020/05/08/andrew-cuomo-eric-schmidt-coronavirus-tech-shock-doctrine/ (accessed 31 March 2021).

Latour, Bruno. *Facing Gaia: Eight Lectures on the New Climatic Regime*. Trans. Catherine Porter. Cambridge, UK: Polity Press, 2017.

Latour, Bruno. *Où suis-je? Leçons du confinement à l'usage des terrestres*. Paris: La Découverte, 2021.

Latour, Bruno. 'What Protective Measures Can You Think of so We Don't Go Back to the Pre-crisis Production Model?' Trans. Stephen Muecke. Bruno Latour, 2020. Available online: http://www.bruno-latour.fr/node/853.html (accessed 31 March 2021).

Latour, Bruno. 'Bruno Latour: "This is a global catastrophe that has come from within"' (interview conducted by Jonathan Watts). *The Guardian*, 6 June 2020. Available online: https://www.theguardian.com/world/2020/jun/06/bruno-latour-coronavirus-gaia-hypothesis-climate-crisis (accessed 31 March 2021).

Levin, David J. *Unsettling Opera: Staging Mozart, Verdi, Wagner, and Zemlinsky*. Chicago: University of Chicago Press, 2007.

Lukács, György. *History and Class Consciousness: Studies in Marxist Dialectics*. Trans. Rodney Livingstone. Cambridge, MA: MIT Press, 1971.

Maia, Tomás. 'O comum dos mortais (pensar a quarentena mundial)'. *Revista Dobra*, Desdobramento pandemia, 2020.

Malabou, Catherine. 'To Quarantine from Quarantine: Rousseau, Robinson Crusoe, and "I"'. *Critical Inquiry* 47, no. 2 (Winter 2021). Originally posted on the Critical Inquiry Blog. Available online: https://critinq.wordpress.com/2020/03/23/to-quarantine-from-quarantine-rousseau-robinson-crusoe-and-i/ (accessed 31 March 2021).

Marx, Karl. *Grundrisse*. Trans. Ben Fowkes. Harmondsworth: Penguin, 1993.

Marx, Karl. 'Theses on Feuerbach'. Trans. Loyd D. Easton and Kurt H. Guddat. In *Selected Writings*, edited by Lawrence H. Simon, 98–101. Indianapolis, IN and Cambridge, MA: Hackett, 1994.

Mbembe, Achille. *Necropolitics*. Trans. Steven Corcoran. Durham, NC and London: Duke University Press, 2019.

Mbembe, Achille. 'The Universal Right to Breathe'. Trans. Carolyn Shread. *Critical Inquiry* 47, no. 2 (Winter 2021). Originally posted on the Critical Inquiry Blog. Available online: https://critinq.wordpress.com/2020/04/13/the-universal-right-to-breathe/ (accessed 15 July 2021).

McBurney, Simon. 'The Encounter: Simon McBurney on an Amazonian Voyage that Exploded Time'. *The Guardian*, 11 February 2016. Available online: https://www.theguardian.com/stage/2016/feb/11/the-encounter-simon-mcburney-barbican-amazon-beaming-petru-popescu-loren-mcintyre (accessed 12 May 2020).

McLuhan, Marshall. *Understanding Media: The Extensions of Man*. With an introduction by Lewis H. Lapham. Cambridge, MA and London: MIT Press, 1994.

Mendonça, José Tolentino. 'Redescobrir o poder da esperança'. *Expresso*, 22 March 2020.

Milner, Yeshimabeit and Amy Traub. 'Data Capitalism and Algorithmic Racism'. Data for Black Lives/Demos, 2021. Available online: https://www.demos.org/research/data-capitalism-and-algorithmic-racism#What-is-Data-Capitalism? (accessed 1 July 2021).

Moten, Fred and Stefano Harney, 'When We Are Apart We Are Not Alone' (interview conducted by Zach Ngin, Sara Van Horn and Alex Westfall). *The College Hill Independent* 40, no. 10 (1 May 2020).

Nancy, Jean-Luc. 'Communovirus' (originally published in *Libération* on 25 March 2020). Trans. David Fernbach. Verso [blog], 27 March 2020. Available online: https://www.versobooks.com/blogs/4626-communovirus (accessed 31 March 2021).

Nietzsche, Friedrich. *On the Genealogy of Morality*. Ed. Keith Ansell-Pearson. Trans. Carol Diethe. Cambridge: Cambridge University Press, 2006.

Noys, Benjamin. *Malign Velocities: Accelerationism and Capitalism*. Winchester, UK and Washington, DC: Zero Books, 2014.

Phelan, Peggy. *Unmarked: The Politics of Performance*. London: Routledge, 1993.

Preciado, Paul B. *Countersexual Manifesto*. Trans. Kevin Gerry Dunn. New York: Columbia University Press, 2018.

Preciado, Paul B. 'Learning from the Virus'. Trans. Molly Stevens. Art Forum, May/June 2020. Available online: https://www.artforum.com/print/202005/paul-b-preciado-82823 (accessed 25 March 2021).

Proust, Marcel. *The Guermantes Way & Cities of the Plain*, vol. 2, *Remembrance of Things Past*. Trans. C. K. Scott Moncrieff and Terence Kilmartin. New York: Random House, 1981.

Py, Olivier. 'La liturgie du théâtre n'a aucune différence avec celle de la messe' (conversation with Anne-Laure Filhol). *La vie*, 29 June 2020. Available online: https://www.lavie.fr/ma-vie/culture/olivier-py-la-liturgie-du-theatre-na-aucune-difference-avec-celle-de-la-messe-1922.php (accessed 1 June 2021).

Rancière, Jacques. *The Ignorant Schoolmaster: Five Lessons in Intellectual Emancipation*. Trans. Kristin Ross. Stanford, CA: Stanford University Press, 1991.

Rancière, Jacques. *Aesthetics and Its Discontents*, trans. Steven Corcoran. Cambridge, UK: Polity Press, 2009.

Rancière, Jacques. *The Emancipated Spectator*. Trans. Gregory Elliott. London: Verso, 2009.

Rancière, Jacques. 'Uma boa oportunidade?' Trans. Peter Pál Perbart. N-1 edições. Available online: https://www.n-1edicoes.org/textos/72 (accessed 31 March 2021).

Rhodes, John. 'Ingenious Performance of *Boris Godunov* at Zurich Opera, Current Envy of the Operatic World'. *Seen and Heard International*, 22 September 2020. Available online: https://seenandheard-international.com/2020/09/ingenious-performance-of-boris-godunov-at-zurich-opera-current-envy-of-the-operatic-world/ (accessed 15 July 2021).

Ricœur, Paul. *Freud and Philosophy: An Essay on Interpretation*. Trans. Denis Savage. New Haven, CT and London: Yale University Press, 1970.

Rosa, Harmut. *Unverfügbarkeit*. Salzburg: Residenz, 2018.

Safatle, Vladimir. 'Para além da necropolítica'. *Pandemia Crítica*. N-1 edições, 2020. Available online: https://www.n-1edicoes.org/textos/191 (accessed 31 March 2021).

Servidei, Laura. 'Technology to the Rescue in Zurich's New Stagings of *Boris Godunov*'. *Backtrack*, 22 September 2020. Available online: https://bachtrack.com/es_ES/review-boris-godunov-kosky-karabits-volle-zurich-september-2020 (accessed 15 July 2021).

Simanowski, Roberto. *Data Love: The Seduction and Betrayal of Digital Technologies*. New York: Columbia University Press, 2016.

Sloterdijk, Peter. *You Must Change Your Life: On Anthropotechnics*. Trans. Wieland Hoban. Cambridge, UK: Polity Press, 2013.

Sloterdijk, Peter. 'Co-Immunism in the Age of Pandemics and Climate Change' (interview conducted by Nathan Gardels). *Noema*, 12 June 2020. Available online: https://www.noemamag.com/co-immunism-an-ethos-for-our-age-of-climate-change/ (accessed 8 July 2021).

Sloterdijk, Peter. 'Humans Are Not Prepared to Protect Nature', *DW*, 23 June 2020. Available online: https://www.dw.com/en/how-do-we-change-peter-sloterdijk-environment-coronavirus-on-the-green-fence-climate-change/a-53533840 (accessed 15 July 2021).

Stengers, Isabelle. *In Catastrophic Times: Resisting the Coming of Barbarism*. Trans. Andrew Goffey. Lüneburg: Meson Press, 2015.

Sterne, Jonathan. *MP3: The Meaning of a Format*. Durham, NC and London: Duke University Press, 2012.

Stiegler, Bernard. *Technics and Time*, vol. 2, *Disorientation*. Trans. Stephen Barker. Stanford, CA: Stanford University Press, 2009.

Stiegler, Bernard. *The Neganthropocene*. Ed., trans. and with an introduction by Daniel Ross. London: Open Humanities Press, 2018.

Stiegler, Bernard. *The Age of Disruption: Technology and Madness in Computational Capitalism*. Trans. Daniel Ross. Cambridge, UK: Polity Press, 2019.

Szendy, Peter. 'Viral Times'. *Critical Inquiry* 47, no. S2 (Winter 2021). Originally posted on the Critical Inquiry blog, 15 April 2020. Available online: https://critinq.wordpress.com/2020/04/15/viral-times/ (accessed 31 March 2021).

Szendy, Peter. 'Pandemia, Ademia, Iconodemia'. Polemology [blog], 31 May 2021. Available online: https://polemologistblog.home.blog/2021/05/31/peter-szendy-pandemia-ademia-iconodemia/ (accessed 20 July 2021).

Tim, 'Tinder and the Absent Date: The Modern Dating Philosophy'. *Philosophy & Philosophers*, 15 February 2015. Available online: https://www.the-philosophy.com/tinder-absent-date-modern-dating-philosophy (accessed 15 July 2021).

Valéry, Paul. *Œuvres*, vol. 2, *Pièces sur l'art*. Paris: Gallimard, 1960.

Virilio, Paul. *Negative Horizon: An Essay in Dromoscopy*. Trans. Michael Degener. London: Continuum, 2005.

Williams, Alex and Nick Srnicek. '#Accelerate: Manifesto for an Accelerationist Politics'. In #*Acelerate: The Accelerationist Reader*, edited by Robin Mackay and Armen Avanessian, 347–62. Falmouth: Urbanomic, 2017.

World Health Organization (WHO). 'WHO Coronavirus (COVID-19): Overview'. Available online: https://covid19.who.int/ (accessed 14 November 2021).

Žižek, Slavoj. *Pandemic!: COVID-19 Shakes the World*. London and New York: OR Books, 2020.

Žižek, Slavoj. *Pandemic! 2: Chronicles of a Time Lost*. London and New York: OR Books, 2020.

Zuboff, Shoshana. *Surveillance Capitalism: The Fight for a Human Future at the New Frontier of Power*. New York: Public Affairs, 2019.

INDEX